United Nations Office at Vienna
Centre for Social Development and Humanitarian Affairs

Violence against Women in the Family

United Nations, New York, 1989

The designations employed and the presentation of material in this publication do not imply the expression of any opinion whatsoever on the part of the Secretariat of the United Nations concerning the legal status of any country, territory, city of area or of its authorities, or concerning the delimitation of its frontiers of boundaries.

ST/CSDHA/2

UNITED NATIONS PUBLICATIONS
Sales No. E.89.IV.5

ISBN: 92-1-130133-5

PREFACE

The Nairobi Forward-looking Strategies for the Advancement of Women to the Year 2000 1/ reflect the international community's recognition that violence against women exists in various forms in everyday life in all societies. They point out that violence against women is a major obstacle to the achievement of peace and the other objectives of the United Nations Decade for Women: Equality, Development and Peace, and that women victims of violence should be given particular attention and comprehensive assistance. They call for the formulation of legal measures for the prevention of violence and for the establishment of national machinery to deal with the question of violence against women within the family and society.

Economic and Social Council resolution 1984/14 of 24 May 1984 on violence in the family requests that work on the subject be included in the programme budget for the biennium 1986-1987 of the Branch for the Advancement of Women, Centre for Social Development and Humanitarian Affairs of the United Nations at Vienna. This included the organization of an Expert Group Meeting on Violence in the Family, with Special Emphasis on its Effects on Women, held at Vienna, from 8 to 12 December 1986. It also included the preparation of the present publication, which attempts to survey available literature and analyse research findings on the issue of violence against women in the family.

The present publication was prepared by a consultant in 1987 under the guidance of the Division for the Advancement of Women, Centre for Social Development and Humanitarian Affairs of the United Nations Office at Vienna and on the basis of the following:

(a) Results of the above-mentioned expert group meeting for which the following had been prepared: 15 case studies (2 from Africa: Egypt, Nigeria; 6 from Asia and the Pacific: Australia, Bangladesh, China, India, Malaysia and Thailand; 1 from Latin America and the Caribbean: Trinidad and Tobago; 3 from Europe: Austria, Greece and the United Kingdom of Great Britain and Northern Ireland; 2 from North America: Canada and the United States of America; and 1 from Western Asia: Kuwait); 5 background papers (1 prepared by the Secretariat and 1 on each of the following countries: Bangladesh, Italy, the Union of Soviet Socialist Republics and the United States of America); and 3 information papers: from Czechoslovakia, France and Norway;

(b) Fifteen case studies commissioned especially for this publication, many of which were expanded versions of case studies prepared for the Expert Group Meeting: 4 from Africa: Egypt, Kenya, Nigeria and Uganda; 5 from Asia and the Pacific: Australia, Bangladesh, Malaysia, Samoa and Thailand; 3 from Latin America and the Caribbean: Brazil, Chile and Colombia; 2 from Europe: Greece, Poland; and 1 from North America: Canada;

(c) Relevant publications by the United Nations system, inter-governmental and non-governmental organizations, as well as literature published in English surveyed by the consultant.

The publication intends to provide an overall picture of violence against women in the family as a world issue rather than as an issue that is confined to one country or cultural system by examining current research on the subject.

It also attempts to identify gaps in knowledge of the issue, which constitute obstacles to the development of a proper understanding of the problem and appropriate action for its eradication.

This publication is intended to contribute to promoting systematic international co-operation in coping with the problem as one of the major obstacles to the implementation of the provisions contained in the Nairobi Forward- looking Strategies and the Convention on the Elimination of All Forms of Discrimination against Women (General Assembly resolution 34/180 of 18 December 1979).

Gratitude is expressed to the Government of Norway, which provided financial resources for the preparation and printing of the study. The study was prepared by Ms. Jane Frances Connors, lecturer in law at the School of Oriental and African Studies, University of London.

Note

1/ Report of the World Conference to Review and Appraise the Achievements of the United Nations Decade for Women: Equality, Development and Peace, Nairobi, 15-26 July 1985 (United Nations publication, Sales No. E.85.IV.10), p. 60, para. 258.

CONTENTS

Part Two

TYPES OF RESPONSE TO VIOLENCE

Part Three

WHAT CAN BE DONE

INTRODUCTION

The twentieth century has seen the development of a concept of human rights, including rights to be free from fear and want, and to be free in speech and thought.

Such human rights have been acknowledged nationally and internationally and guaranteed in domestic laws and constitutions and in international agreements and instruments. The recognition and implementation of human rights at national and international levels have been viewed as essential in the development of not only the individual, but also the nation and, ultimately, the world. Recognition and implementation will lead, it is believed, to equality, development and peace.

Women - over half the world's population, performing two thirds of its work, receiving one tenth of its income and owning less than one hundredth of its property - have been revealed as seriously deprived of basic human rights. Not only are women denied equality with the balance of the world's population, men, but also they are often denied liberty and dignity, and in many situations suffer direct violations of their physical and mental autonomy.

Violence against women has emerged as a serious issue and the subject of world-wide debate. The problem has been recognized internationally and seen as a serious obstacle to development and peace, and its implications for equality are obvious.

Research indicates that violence against women is not confined to violence perpetrated by strangers. Indeed, it has become clear that women are more often at risk from those with whom they live and that many of them live constantly with the threat of "domestic violence", whether battery, rape, incest or emotional abuse. Until recently, however, although it is clear that female victimization within the home has long existed, this violence has been hidden by family privacy, guilt and embarrassment and, to a certain extent, traditional customs and culture.

Studies in family violence are modern. Only a few decades ago, issues such as child abuse, wife beating and incest would have been acknowledged, but not viewed as serious problems. 1/ The problem of child abuse emerged as a serious and pervasive one in the early 1960s, 2/ but wife abuse has appeared as a field of study and concern only within the last 25 years. 3/ Indeed, the World Conference of the International Women's Year held at Mexico City in 1975, although adopting a world plan of action so that women could enjoy equal rights, opportunities and responsibilities and could contribute to the development process on equal terms with men, laid no stress on violence against women in the family, stating only that adequate family counselling services should be set up wherever possible and family courts staffed with personnel, including women, who were trained in law as well as other disciplines in order to assist in the solution of conflicts arising among members of families. 4/

Further, while the issue of violence against women was noted as being a matter of serious concern at international meetings, 5/ it was not until 1980 that the increasing public awareness of the need to eliminate all forms of violence against women and children, including domestic violence, was fully reflected when the World Conference of the United Nations Decade for Women: Equality, Development and Peace, held at Copenhagen, stated that domestic violence was a complex problem and constituted an intolerable offence to the dignity of human beings. 6/ Accordingly, the Programme of Action for the Second Half of the United Nations Decade for Women, adopted at the Copenhagen

World Conference, advocated research into the extent and causes of domestic violence with a view to its elimination and the provision of effective help, such as the establishment of centres for treatment, shelter and counselling for women who were the victims of violence. 7/

The concern of the international community with respect to violence against women in the home has been manifested at various meetings following the Copenhagen World Conference. Thus, for example, the issue was intensively discussed by the Commission on the Status of Women and the Committee on Crime Prevention and Control at their sessions in 1982 and 1984, which ultimately led to the adoption by the Economic and Social Council of resolutions 1982/22 on abuses against women and children, 1984/14 on violence in the family and one of women as victims. The issue received increasing attention in 1984 and 1985, particularly during the preparatory meetings for the Nairobi World Conference to Review and Appraise the Achievements of the United Nations Decade for Women: Equality, Development and Peace and the Seventh United Nations Congress on the Prevention of Crime and Treatment of Offenders, both of which took place in 1985.

Violence against women in the family was acknowledged in the Nairobi Forward-looking Strategies 8/ to be a complex issue and a major obstacle to the achievement of peace and the other objectives of the United Nations Decade for Women, which were equality and development, while the Seventh United Nations Congress adopted resolution 6 on the fair treatment of women by the criminal justice system. 9/ Interest in the issue culminated in the adoption by the General Assembly of the United Nations of resolution 40/36 of 29 November 1985 on domestic violence, which advocated concerted and multi-disciplinary action within and outside the United Nations system to combat the problem and urged the introduction of specific criminological measures to achieve the fair and humane response of justice systems to the victimization of women in the family. 10/

The initiatives of the United Nations were reflected by parallel interest in other international forums. The First Commonwealth Meeting of Ministers for Women's Affairs, held at Nairobi, in 1985, expressed concern at the pervasiveness of violence against women in the family, as did the Council of Europe, 11/ also, non-governmental institutions, individually and collectively, have been campaigning in the area. 12/

The work of the United Nations culminated in late 1986 with the Expert Group Meeting on Violence in the Family with Special Emphasis on its Effects on Women. This Meeting, which was organized by the Branch for the Advancement of Women and the Crime Prevention and Criminal Justice Branch, both of the Centre for Social Development and Humanitarian Affairs, United Nations Office at Vienna, brought together experts from all regions of the world. It examined the various aspects of violence against women in the family in order to obtain a better understanding of the causes, nature and effects of such violence and coercion. Further, it considered current methods of crisis intervention and assistance available to victims. The Meeting made recommendations for concrete and immediate measures to confront violence against women in the home and long-term preventative measures aimed at improving the status of women and at ensuring a more accessible, sensitive, effective and fair response by civil and criminal justice systems to the victimization of women in the family. 13/

Violence against women in the family has thus been recognized as a priority area for international and national action. It is an issue that affects all countries and cultures. All the research evidence that is available suggests that violence against women in the home is a universal problem, occurring across all cultures and in all countries.

Although the study is written from the perspective that the problem is a universal one, it is necessary to acknowledge that certain difficulties have been encountered in the attempt to survey the problem from a cross-cultural and cross-country perspective. Foremost among these is the fact that violence against women in the home has emerged as a serious issue only in the last 25 years and thus the available research material is new. This material indicates that much remains to be understood about the nature, extent and treatment of family violence. Unequivocally, the available studies reveal that a major problem exists, but they are too imprecise to answer questions on who is most at risk and how resources can be allocated most effectively. The information on treatment programmes is fragmentary: certain types of intervention appear to be effective, but much more information is required. The long-term effects of family violence remain a patchwork of data and speculation.

The second problem is the fact that most research into violence against women in the family has emerged from Western Europe, North America, Australia and New Zealand. Few studies have been undertaken in Eastern Europe, and even fewer in the developing countries. Indeed, it is perhaps safe to say that the only comprehensive and systematic study of violence against women in the home that has been undertaken in a developing country is of Papua New Guinea. 14/ In view of this, any study that attempts to take a cross-cultural approach to the issue must acknowledge that the data is predominantly Western.

The third problem is the question of the definition of violence itself. In this context, it is apparent that the definition of violence may differ from individual to individual, from country to country and from cultural context to cultural context. Thus, for example, it may be suggested that verbal or emotional violence is not violence in a particular cultural context, while it may be regarded as such in another cultural milieu. Again, it may be suggested that certain cultures tolerate, or even expect, a certain level of physical violence in intimate relationships. 15/ The question is, ultimately, whether there can be a common definition of violence that can be applied across cultures, or whether violence is something that can be defined only against the backdrop of culture, tradition and custom.

While the difficulties of cross-cultural research and analysis must be acknowledged, so too must be the advantages of such an approach given the particular subject. Certainly, if a common thread emerges across cultures, greater understanding of domestic violence against women will be achieved. This, in turn, will create a solid basis for both short-term and long-term strategies to confront the violence.

The work that follows is the result of research into literature pertaining to violence against women in the home. Primarily it is concerned with the physical and mental abuse of women by their husbands or lovers, although it does touch upon abuse by other family members and upon abuses against other women in the family. Thus, for example, it will touch, although not greatly, upon the sexual abuse of female children in the family. The main concern of the work is, however, what is called popularly "wife battery" or sometimes "domestic violence".

The available research literature concerning the problem of wife abuse has been augmented by case studies prepared by experts in various regions of the world, particularly in the developing world, so that the Western bias in the current research is avoided to a certain extent. None the less, the analysis remains more Western than cross-cultural, a fact that is explained by the limitations and the dearth of material available from developing or Eastern European countries.

The paper has been divided into three parts. Part one provides the context of the study. It surveys the definition of the subject, the incidence, the results of the problem and the causes of the conduct. It concludes that the problem is a serious one in terms of incidence and sequelae, but acknowledges that research into the aetiology of maltreatment has not produced a definitive and unanimously accepted dynamic of the behaviour. Part two describes the current responses to the issue. As the eradication of the problem has been seen as one essentially requiring legal measures, this part concentrates on the legal responses that have been utilized, while it also surveys the response of the health, welfare and community sectors. Part three attempts to draw conclusions from the previous parts. It seeks to recommend both short-term and long-term strategies to confront the problem of violence against women in the home. Primarily, however, it attempts to pinpoint particular gaps in the current knowledge of the issue. As such, therefore, it seeks to establish priority areas for action and research.

Notes

1/ W. Brienes and L. Gordon, "The new scholarship on family violence", Signs, No. 8, 1983, p. 490.

2/ Ibid., p. 493.

3/ Ibid., p. 507.

4/ Report of the World Conference of the International Women's Year, Mexico City, 19 June-2 July 1975 (United Nations publication, Sales No. E.76.IV.1), chap. II, sect. A, para. 131.

5/ See, for example, Fifth United Nations Congress on the Prevention of Crime and the Treatment of Offenders, Geneva, 1-12 September 1975 (United Nations publication, Sales No. E.76.IV.2) which noted that sexual assault was becoming more prevalent.

6/ Report of the World Conference of the United Nations Decade for Women: Equality, Development and Peace, Copenhagen, 14 to 30 July 1980 (United Nations publication, Sales No. E.80.IV.3 and Corrigendum), chap. I, sect. A, paras. 141-164.

7/ Ibid., para. 163.

8/ Report of the World Conference to Review and Appraise the Achievements of the United Nations Decade for Women: Equality, Development and Peace, Nairobi, 15-26 July 1985 (United Nations publication, Sales No. E.85.IV.10).

9/ Seventh United Nations Congress on the Prevention of Crime and the Treatment of Offenders, Milan, 25 August-6 September 1985 (United Nations publication, Sales No. E.86.IV.1), chap. IV, sect. C, para. 229.

10/ General Assembly resolution 40/35 which calls for the development of standards for the prevention of juvenile delinquency "recognizing that the prevention of juvenile delinquency includes measure for the protection of juveniles who are abandoned, neglected, abused and in marginal circumstances, and, in general, those who are at social risk" and resolution 40/34 adopting the Declaration of Basic Principles of Justice for Victims of Crime and Abuse of Power are both applicable to the general situation of women as victims of crime.

- 7 -

11/ The Council of Europe held a Colloquy on Violence within the Family: Measures in the Social Field, from 25 to 27 November 1987, at Strasbourg.

12/ For example, the International Society of Criminology and the International Alliance of Women held meetings at the same time as the Seventh United Nations Congress on the Prevention of Crime and Treatment of Offenders in 1985.

13/ Report of the Expert Group Meeting on Violence in the Family with Special Emphasis on its Effects on Women, Vienna, 8-12 December 1986.

14/ The Law Reform Commission of Papua New Guinea has produced four publications on the problem of violence against women in the home. These are discussed in the body of the work.

15/ K. A. Long, "Cultural considerations in the assessment and treatment of intrafamilial abuse", American Journal of Orthopsychiatry, No. 56, 1986, p. 131.

Part One

VIOLENCE IN THE FAMILY: CAUSES AND CONSEQUENCES

In all countries and cultures, women have frequently been the victims of abuse by their intimates. 1/ They have been battered, sexually abused and psychologically injured by persons with whom they should enjoy the closest trust. This maltreatment has gone largely unpunished, unremarked and has even been tacitly, if not explicitly, condoned. 2/

Legal systems, which are a reflection of cultural values, often gave a husband the right to chastise, or even kill his wife, if she was regarded as sufficiently disobedient. Blackstone in his Commentaries on the Laws of England (1775), for example, stated that the husband was empowered to correct the wife "in the same moderation that a man is allowed to correct his apprentice or children". 3/ This power was confirmed in judicial decisions in England and North America, 4/ where the domestic chastisement of a wife went unpunished unless some permanent injury resulted from the husband's violence. 5/ Even where permanent injury or death resulted, the husband's actions were often justified on the grounds of, for example, provocation 6/ and any penalty he received was always light. 7/ The husband's right to chastise his wife received acceptance in popular culture by being known as the "rule of thumb", because it appeared that normal wife beating involved chastisement with a stick no bigger than a man's thumb. 8/

Husbands were also given the right to sexually abuse their wives, a right that was again reflected in legal institutions. Thus, in many systems, husbands were given the right to bring actions against anyone who committed adultery with or seduced their wives 9/ and were not subject to sanction if they forced their wives to have sexual intercourse. Hence, John Stuart Mill in the Subjection of Women remarked: "... the wife: however brutal a tyrant she may unfortunately be chained to - though she may know that he hates her, though it may be his daily pleasure to torture her, and though she may feel it impossible not to loathe him - can claim from her and enforce the lowest degradation of a human being, that of being made the instrument of an animal function contrary to her inclinations". 10/

These legal structures merely mirrored the general view of most societies, that a wife was subordinate to and the property of her husband and therefore was to be treated as he saw fit and, indeed, punished if disobedient. This view went hand-in-hand with a general philosophy that the dynamics of a particular family acting within this socially accepted structure were private and, therefore, were to be interfered with only unusually and, certainly, rarely on behalf of the wife.

Given this general view, which fostered the toleration of violence against women by, in particular, their male intimates, the "discovery" that women were the subject of abuse within the family was delayed. Occasionally liberal philosophers 11/ and early feminists 12/ drew attention to the fact that women were victimized in their families, but it was not until the 1970s that large-scale campaigns confronting the issue were launched. These campaigns, which owe their impetus to the renaissance of the feminist movement in the 1960s, began in Europe 13/ and North America, 14/ but quickly spread to other areas of the world. 15/ They have been responsible for the establishment of hundreds of shelters and other services for battered women and their children, and for placing what was once a private individual family problem on the national and international agenda.

Although violence against women in the family is now acknowledged to be a serious problem both in incidence and sequelae in most countries of the world, and much research into the problem has been undertaken in the last 15 years, there are still serious gaps in our knowledge of the issue.

As noted earlier, most of the research into family violence and, indeed, most particularly, violence against women in the family has been undertaken in the Western European countries, North America, Australia and New Zealand. Few studies have emerged from developing countries and most of them have been under-funded and, therefore, could not have been comprehensive. Indeed, much of the information pertaining to developing countries that is offered in the present study is based on the case studies prepared by experts for the Seminar on Violence in the Family. Some of these case studies were the first research projects into the problem in the country concerned.

Nothwithstanding this caveat, the evidence that exists suggests that violence against women in the home, which may have various manifestations and extremely grave short and long-term results, is a serious and widespread problem and exists in various forms in everyday life in all societies. Moreover, evidence suggests that the risk of violence and violation within the household is one thing women, irrespective of their social position, creed, colour or culture, share in common.

I. MANIFESTATIONS OF VIOLENCE IN THE FAMILY

The manifestations of violence against women in the family are many and varied. Women may become the target for abuse in their roles of wife, mother, daughter-in-law, sister, sister-in-law, lover, ex-wife or ex-lover. Further, in extended families or families with domestic servants, other women may become victims of maltreatment. Most commonly, and this is so in all cultures, the perpetrators of the abuse are the men of the family, be they the husband, ex-husband, lover, ex-lover, father, father-in-law, uncle, brother or step-brother of the woman. 16/

The establishment of appropriate shortand long-term services for vulnerable categories of female victims and the ultimate eradication of abuse within the family depend upon a definition of the objectionable conduct. For the definition to be comprehensive, it must include a description of "violence against women in the family", an indication of the scope of the family, and of the usual victims and perpetrators of such violence.

A. Conduct

Research indicates that violence against women in the home takes various forms. At its most basic level, it consists of physical violence or aggressive behaviour towards the victim's body. It can include pushing, pinching, spitting, kicking, pulling the woman's hair, hitting, punching, choking, burning, clubbing, stabbing, throwing acid or boiling water, or shooting. It can range from minor bruising to murder, often beginning with what could be regarded as trivial contacts and then escalating into more frequent and serious attacks. Physical attack is often accompanied by, or culminates in, sexual violence wherein the victim is forced to have sexual intercourse with her assailant or take part in unwanted sexual activity. 17/ Such physical attack may also involve specific attacks on the breasts or genitals. Frequently, where physical attack occurs during pregnancy, it is often directed at the woman's stomach 18/ and may result in miscarriage.

At a more sophisticated level, violence against women in the home may be manifested by psychological or mental violence that includes constant verbal abuse, harassment, excessive possessiveness, isolation and deprivation of physical and economic resources. Thus, isolating the woman from her family and friends, restricting her access to the family income, degrading and belittling her verbally, either when alone or in front of her children, family or friends, and threatening her with violence or murder or suicide, or taunting her with threats of divorce, intentions of taking another wife or deportation if her residence permit is not in order or depends on the continuance of the relationship, fall within the definition of violence. So also will denial of sexual contact or activity resulting in sexual frustration, self doubt and guilt about her sexual attractiveness. Finally, violent activity, not directed at her, such as destruction of her property or pets, falls within the definition.

In sum, therefore, conduct that falls within the definition of violence against women in the family includes physical battering, sexual battering and psychological battering. In an abusive relationship, the woman may be subject to all forms of violence - physical, sexual and psychological - or she may be subject to one manifestation only. Whatever form she is subjected to, she will run the risk of physical or psychic harm.

While violence may take these various forms, it is not to be concluded that isolated behaviour comes within the definition. Although distressing and regrettable, minor incidents or objectionable behaviour probably occur within most intimate relationships. Thus, while all such behaviour is condemned, it is the persistence of such violence that establishes it as coming within the definition. Certainly, an isolated attack with serious consequences falls within the definition, but the particular concern of this work is systematic and frequent physical, sexual or psychological abuse.

B. Victims and assailants: who victimizes whom

The term "family" suggests safety and security, a private haven or shelter from the pressures and difficulties of the world outside, a place where its members are able to co-exist in security and harmony. Modern studies suggest, however, that far from being a place of safety, the family can be "cradle of violence" and that much of this violence is directed at the female members of the family, in particular, those females who have the role of wife, and that the most likely perpetrator of this violence will be her husband. 19/

Certainly, there are other victims of abuse. Young girls and children are victims of sexual assault within the family, as to a lesser extent are young boys. 20/ This pattern is not limited to industrialized countries, Jamaican and Samoan figures, for example, indicate that there is a significant amount of sexual abuse of young women within the family. 21/ Elderly family members, particularly elderly women, are vulnerable to their grown-up children, 22/ as are young children, 23/ and sick and infirm family members. In polygamous households, co-wives assault fellow wives, 24/ and in the extended family, female members are often at risk from both male and female relatives. 25/ Further, female domestic servants are at risk from their female employers and from the male members of the employing family. 26/ None the less, much violence is directed at the wife, and this violence is directed at her in her role as wife. Indeed, even where such violence is perpetrated by someone other than her spouse, for example, her mother-in-law in order to extract greater dowry payments from her natal family, 26/ such violence will frequently stem from the same root: her inferior status and subjugation as a wife, which makes her victimization socially tolerable.

Controversy exists about the extent to which men are also victimized in the home. Shortly after the publication of studies in the United States which revealed that many women were repeatedly abused by their partners, 27/ a number of articles appeared, in the main authored by Suzanne Steinmetz of the Straus, Gelles and Steinmetz team, suggesting that husband battering was common and indeed could be the most underreported type of family violence. 28/ The concept of a wife terrorizing and battering her husband attracted wide media coverage. Time Magazine, for example, which had previously only carried a few paragraphs on wife abuse, devoted a full page to the issue in 1978. 29/ Published estimates of the amount of victimization of husbands by their wives within the home were quickly exaggerated, 30/ so that one report suggested that 20 million American husbands were abused by their wives.

The "battered husband syndrome" confused the issue of wife abuse and was able to give substance to opposition to the movement to aid battered wives. 31/ Research was, therefore, initiated to ascertain whether husband battery was indeed as common as Steinmetz had suggested and, if so, whether its results were as serious as wife battery. Almost all writers concluded, on re-examination of the issue, that while women could be violent to their husbands, such violence was not as common as violence by husbands towards their wives 32/ where wives were violent this violence was usually in self defence 33/ and, certainly, rarely resulted in serious injury and was fre- quently not repeated. 34/ Statistics from Poland reveal that in 95-98 per cent of domestic violence cases, the victims are women, 35/ and a Thai survey of 24 newspaper reports of violence within the home showed that 16 of the victims were women, while in those cases where the men were victims, their victimization resulted from the fact that the women fought back. 36/

Studies can, therefore, and do, reveal high rates of violence by wives against their husbands. Critical assessment of these results indicates, however, that wives are victimized in the family to a much greater extent than husbands and as such deserve to be the focus of the most immediate remedial steps. 37/ This is not to say, however, that violence by women against their husbands is something to be ignored because of the even greater violence perpetrated by husbands. Violent female behaviour does occur and must be confronted through proper understanding of its nature and causes, so that strategies can be introduced to eliminate such violence. 38/

C. Characteristics of victims and abusers: class, culture and age

While studies indicate that episodes of violence by the husband against the wife exist in as many as one in three marriages in certain communities 39/ and assertions are made that such violence is class, colour and culture blind, 40/ little is known of the precise prevalence of violence against women in the home in the general population. Moreover, there is a paucity of information on the social characteristics, such as age, class, culture and ethnic origin, of abused wives and their partners. Certainly, evidence of the existence of wife abuse comes from all countries and societies 41/ and from all classes and backgrounds, but much of this tends to be unsystematic and anecdotal.

There are a number of reasons for this. Marital violence is largely a hidden problem, causing much shame and subterfuge. Moreoever, even where it is identified, little information is collected, particularly in developing countries. Further, the usual sources of information on violence against wives tend to lead to conclusions that may not be totally accurate. Thus, for example, there is an overrepresentation in the literature of victims who are economically disadvantaged or who could be described as lower class. 42/ United States studies reveal an overrepresentation of victims who are black or in receipt of welfare benefits, 43/ while statistics from Nigeria indicate that the victims are likely to be from polygamous households that are economically disadvantaged. 44/ Again, victims are revealed to be younger, rather than middle aged or old. 45/ In this way, a profile of a typical battered woman emerges who is young, working class and perhaps, if such is available, on welfare.

Care must be taken with this profile as it may be the result of available research samples, such as population in women's refuges, and public hospital and social work records, which may result in skewed information. A middleor upper-class woman is likely to have more options available to her than a working-class woman and thus, for example, may not be forced to use a woman's refuge. 46/ Further, public hospitals are used primarily by the economically disadvantaged, with the wealthy able to use private doctors and hospitals that are less open to researchers. Finally, social work or welfare records attract information pertaining to less privileged groups, the poor being more likely to come to the attention of government officials as the upper classes are able, usually, to insulate themselves from the supervision of the welfare system. In sum, the profile of the typical battered woman may become the result of the available visible research material. Thus, anecdotal material and small research samples become crucial to support the assertion that wife abuse crosses all cultures, classes, creeds and colours.

While evidence exists to indicate that wife abuse occurs at all levels of
society, 47/ no evidence suggests that the conduct is distributed equally
among all groups in society. For example, there is some evidence to suggest
that rural women are at greater risk than urban women, a survey undertaken in
Bangladesh revealing that women were victimized more in the villages than in
the urban centres 48/ and it well may be that there is more wife abuse in
families with lower incomes 49/ or where the husband has received less education. However, despite variations that may exist, all research has produced
the key result that violence against wives is prevalent throughout the economic and social structure and appears to have no cultural barriers. All that
can be said is that there is no typical victim of abuse and no typical perpetrator, except in so far as the victim is, overwhelmingly, female and the
perpetrator male.

D. Conclusion

Violence against women in the home can, therefore, be defined as violence
perpetrated by a man upon a woman in the domestic sphere. It is not confined
to legally married couples, but extends to cover couples who are cohabiting or
couples who are living apart. It also covers women who may be the subject of
violence from male relatives or friends or agents of the husband, such as his
mother or other wife. For the purposes of this study, the definition does
not, however, extend to include other forms of family violence such as child
abuse, child sexual abuse, or abuse of elderly and disabled relatives in the
home, problems that are none the less acknowledged as serious and requiring
study. It is, therefore, primarily concerned with abuse by "husbands" of
"wives" (married or unmarried): that is, where there is some element of con-
jugality, but not necessarily of cohabitation, and where the relationship
should be one of equality or one between peers. Violence is defined widely,
to include physical, sexual and psychological acts, as is the family, so as
to include extended family and polygamous systems.

Finally, as the definition concerns abuse by husbands of wives, accurate
terminology to describe the conduct is critical. In the literature, violence
against women by their partners is variously termed spouse abuse, marital
violence, domestic dispute, domestic violence and family violence. Such terms
are misleading because all evidence suggests that the problem is not one of
spouse abuse, but rather of wife abuse. Neutral terms obscure the issue, hide
the connection between battering and male supremacy, and suggest that women
are as much to blame for the violence as are men. 50/ So also is the term
"battered wives" misleading. As one researcher cogently remarks, it is "as
though the problem of international terrorists hijacking aeroplanes was described as the 'problem of hostages'". 51/ In other words, the term "battered
wives" serves again to shift the emphasis from the instigators of the violence
to the victims of the violence, making it a short step to lay the blame for
the problem and encourage the search for solutions against the victims rather
than the perpetrators. 51/ In short, the issue is one of violent husbands and
wife assault or wife abuse. As such, the terms "wife assault" or "wife abuse"
perhaps most accurately and adequately describe the nature and direction of
the activity.

II. HOW MUCH VIOLENCE EXISTS

The extent of violence against women in the home has been largely hidden and widely denied by communities that fear that an admission of its incidence will be an assault on the integrity of the family. However, existing statistics reflect the pervasiveness, the frequency and the intensity of violence perpetrated against women in the home in all countries of the world.

A reliable statistical estimation of the number of women who are battered by their spouses is crucial for two reasons. The first reason is so that appropriate responses and services can be established to deal with the results of the problem. The second, and more fundamental reason, is that figures indicating the level of domestic violence may go someway to establishing its aetiology. Thus, as Elizabeth Wilson points out:

"If you are one of only 500 women in a population of 50 million then you have certainly been more than unlucky and there may perhaps be something very peculiar about your husband, or unusual about your circumstances, or about you; on the other hand, if you are one of 500,000 women then that suggests something very different - that there is something wrong not with a few individual men, or women, or marriages, but with the situation in which many women and children regularly get assaulted - that situation being the home and the family." 52/

A reliable estimation of the actual level of violence against wives is difficult to establish for a number of reasons.

First, research into wife abuse is relatively new so that up until recently available information was so incomplete and disorganized as to be functionally useless. Research into the issue is particularly new in developing countries, where gender, specific research is in any case fairly uncommon. Thus, while large-scale surveys have been undertaken in countries such as the United States and the United Kingdom, there are no such surveys in most developing countries. However, a number of developing countries have begun survey research in this area. Hence, some figures are now available for Papua New Guinea, 53/ which has embarked on a comprehensive study of the problem, and a few figures are available for Nigeria, Colombia, Bangladesh and Chile. 54/

Secondly, current methods of estimating the statistical level of wife battery are problematic relying, in the main, on reported incidents of abuse in, for example, police, welfare and hospital records, populations in women's refuges or self-reports through phone-ins or field surveys.

Statistics culled from police records and other official sources, while indicating that wife abuse is a problem, notoriously only present the tip of the iceberg. Victims are often very reluctant to report that they have been abused, because of guilt, shame and loyalty. They fear that they may lose the economic support of their husband or harm his career. In particular, victims may be very reluctant to report their problems to the police because they may be of the view that the police response will be negative. 55/ Moreover, even if the victim does make a report, the statistic may be lost because the official fails to record the incident or records the incident in such a fashion that it becomes meaningless for research purposes. Criminal statistics, for example, although they could be a major source of comprehensive data on wife abuse, frequently do not cross-reference the sex of the victim to the sex of her assailant and very often fail to indicate the relationship between victim and offender. In these circumstances, it is impossible to distinguish wife assault from any other crime, and thus wife abuse becomes statistically invisible.

Surveys based on self-reporting are also problematic. Again, women who have been abused may prefer to keep the problem to themselves or, if they do respond, they may tend to overestimate, or more commonly, underestimate the amount of violence they incur. Thus a push or a slap may not appear to be noteworthy enough and hence not be mentioned. Furthermore, the self-report survey may itself limit its data base by its method. For example, if the "phone in" survey method is used, the statistical base is automatically limited to women who have access to a telephone and have verbal confidence. Such a survey tends to rule out information from women from ethnic minorities.

Finally, surveys, in general, can never claim to be fully representative. They are limited by the fact that the way researchers define marital violence is not constant, they rely on other people's perception of interpersonal relations and often lose any claim to be totally representative by excluding various groups from the data base. For example, most surveys are taken of couples who are currently living together, thereby excluding evidence of violence from past marriages, and any survey of a population of women using a refuge is automatically unrepresentative as these women have themselves already defined themselves as battered.

Notwithstanding these problems, statistics which do exist indicate that some degree of violence in the home is common and most frequently, the victims of this violence are women.

A. What statistics show

Criminal and police statistics reveal that violence against women, ranging from assaults to homicide, is a significant pattern within the family in probably all countries of the world. R. E. Dobash and R. Dobash report that in England and Wales for the years 1885 and 1905 out of 487 murders committed by men, 124 - or more than a quarter of the victims - were women murdered by their husbands, while a further 115 were mistresses or girlfriends of their assailants. 56/ Twentieth century official figures for the United Kingdom reveal that this pattern has not changed. 57/ Similar statistics were discovered by Von Hentig 58/ and Wolfgang 59/ who used United States samples. A retrospective study of 170 cases of women murdered in Bangladesh between 1983 and 1985 revealed that 50 per cent of these occurred within the family. 60/

Official statistics on male violence against women other than criminal homicide similarly reveal that the victim is most likely to be the wife and the offender the husband. Hence, the First Report of the British Crime Survey 61/ found that 10 per cent of all assault victims were women who had been assaulted by their present or previous husband or lover. 62/ Furthermore, a comprehensive analysis of recorded incidents of assaults on women in two Scottish cities, carried out by the Dobashes in 1974 revealed that wife assault was the second most common form of violent crime, amounting to 25 per cent of crimes recorded by the police. 63/ Official statistics from Poland also reveal that high levels of violence exist in Polish families, with most of this violence directed by the husband against the wife. 64/

Given the paucity of research into family violence in developing countries, official statistics - police reports and hospital and medical records - usually provide the only numerical records for violence against wives. It is clear that these records reveal that the problem of wife abuse is as great in such countries as in the developed countries. Thus, for example, a survey of police records and medical statistics from two hospitals in Vanuatu revealed that wife abuse was not an uncommon occurrence, 65/ while a Colombian study by Dr. Ana Maria Berenguer of 1,170 cases of bodily injuries in Bogota hospitals revealed that 20 per cent of the cases were due to con-jugal violence, with women being the victims of the assault in 94 per cent of the cases. Similarly, alarming figures emerged from a study by Ximena Ahumada and Ruth Alvarez who reviewed cases that had been seen at a public hospital emergency room and two clinics in Santiago, Chile, where during three months, September, October and November 1986, 10,545 assault cases had been treated, of which 2,618 were cases of women, 1,884 of whom were victims of family violence. 66/

Estimates of the level of violence against wives can also be made by extrapolating from figures culled from divorce courts. Again, studies from the United Kingdom, 67/ Canada 68/ and the United States 69/ indicate that violence by the husband is frequently offered as a ground for divorce, a trend that also exists in Egypt, where divorce petitions to the Cairo Personnel Status Court reveal that a number of women suffer from physical violence and ill-treatment 70/ and Greece. 71/ Similarly, statistics from Jamaica indicate that in 1980, 122 out of 768 divorces were granted on the grounds of cruelty and 25 per cent of the 109 women who sought family counselling in the Social Services Sector of the Family Court in 1982 complained of violence perpetrated against them by their spouses. 72/ Statistics can also be retrieved by examination of court orders excluding one party from the home, if such are available in the jurisdiction. 73/

Similar estimates can be made using the numbers of women who use women's refuges as a base for assessment. Here the fact that the 200 refuges in England and Wales provided places for 11,400 women during the 12 months from September 1977 to September 1978, particularly given that these refuges are seriously overcrowded, suggests a critical and pervasive problem of marital violence. 74/ Large numbers of women in Canada similarly take advantage of refuges or transition houses 75/ and it appears that in any society where such facilities are available, demand by battered women for places in the refuges or transition houses greatly outnumbers the supply. 76/

In a number of countries specific research projects to determine the actual level of violence against wives have been undertaken. Perhaps the best known of these studies is that undertaken by Straus, Steinmetz and Gelles who attempted to determine the level of marital violence in the United States by extrapolating from a survey of 2,143 persons, regarded as nationally represen-tative, who were living in intact marital relationships. In order to make this extrapolation, the research team administered a test called the Conflict Tactics Scales, which investigated the conflicts that family members had had during the previous year and the methods by which the conflicts had been resolved. Resolution was measured on a continuum of eight acts ranging from non-violent tactics - calm discussion, to most violent - using a knife or a gun. While the survey was limited in that it did not investigate the events preceding or following each act, failed to determine the severity of the injuries, if any, suffered by the victim and only focused on 1975, it revealed that 16 per cent of those surveyed reported marital violence in the year of the survey and 28 per cent at some point during the marriage, allowing the team to extrapolate and conclude that during the 12 months preceding the interview, 3.8 per cent of the women in the United States had been victims of violence in the home. 77/ Straus and Gelles replicated this survey in 1985 and found that compared with the earlier survey, there had been a 27 per cent decrease in incidents of wife beating. None the less, incidence remained extremely high. 78/

Surveys have been undertaken in other countries 79/ and all have emerged with very similar results. A three-year study of violence against women in Austria discovered a high level of wife abuse in Vienna. 80/ Again, few developing countries have undertaken surveys of this nature, but where they have done so the pattern is the same.

Perhaps the most comprehensive surveys undertaken in a developing country have been those by the Papua New Guinea Law Reform Commission, which has surveyed representative samples of a number of tribal groups in both rural and urban parts of Papua New Guinea. These studies indicate that in some areas of the country up to as many as 67 per cent of wives have suffered marital violence. 81/ Other attempts to survey the incidence of the problem have been made in developing countries. Hence, a Kuwaiti researcher has administered a survey to 153 women and 157 men in Kuwait, which revealed that 51 women had suffered from marital violence. 82/ In Kenya and Thailand, researchers have culled newspaper reports and discovered a significant level of violence against women in the home, 83/ and in Nigeria 84/ and Uganda, 85/ where small-scale, largely informal studies have been administered.

B. Conclusion

The numbers of women who are assaulted by their spouses will probably never be known. Investigation so far has centred on official records such as crime statistics, the numbers of divorces requested on grounds of physical cruelty, wife-abuse claims handled by family courts, police and hospital records and the numbers of women using refuge facilities. Further statistical estimation has been based on research specifically geared to discover the number of women who are abused. All of these methods of investigation are problematic.

The figures that do exist, despite the difficulties that beset them, indicate that violence against women in the home is a very common problem in most countries. Further, while little research to reveal the level of wife abuse has been undertaken in developing countries, available evidence suggests that the problem is as great in those societies as in industrialized ones. In sum, therefore, it may be concluded that violence is part of the dynamics of many family situations, women being murdered, assaulted, sexually abused, threatened and humiliated within their own homes by the men to whom they have committed themselves, and that this does not seem to be considered as unusual or uncommon behaviour.

III.   RESULTS OF VIOLENCE AGAINST WOMEN IN THE HOME

Violence against women in the home has both short-term and long-term effects for the individual woman, her children and society in general. It is a conduct that frequently results in severe physical injury, at times culminating in death. Moreover, the syndrome leads to multiple medical and psychological sequelae for her. 86/ Studies suggest that battered women are far more likely to have unsuccessful pregnancies, often being attacked while pregnant. 86/ Battered women are overrepresented among female alcoholics, drug abusers and women who have mental illness. Suicide is 12 times as likely to have been attempted by a woman who is subject to abuse than by one who has not. 86/

Beyond the short term physical and mental effects that abuse has on the individual woman, such abuse has serious consequences for her self image and that of her abuser. The woman is offered limited chances for progress and development, which in turn has a profound impact on the development of society as a whole as its female members are prevented from exercising their funda- mental rights and creative potential.

Wife battery, furthermore, has negative implications for the stability of marriage, the quality of family life, and the health and socialization of children. Indeed, evidence exists which suggests that child abuse is more common in families where wife battery is present, delinquency and criminality in children in such families may be more frequent and that children of violent marriages are more likely to establish violent families of their own.

A.   Short-term effects: injury to women

At its most basic level, wife battery causes physical injury to the individual woman. This injury can range from bruising to death. Thus, Gayford, reported, from his United States study using 100 women:

"All had received the minimum of bruises, but 44 had also received lacerations of which 17 were due to attack with a sharp instrument such as bottle, knife or razor. Twenty-six had received fractures of nose, teeth or ribs and eight had fractures of other bones, ranging from fingers and arms to jaw and skull. Two had their jaws dislocated and two others had similar injuries to the shoulder. There was evidence of retinal damage in two women and one had epilepsy as a result of her injuries. In 19 cases there were allegations that strangulation attempts had been made. Bruises and scalds occurred in eleven and bites in seven cases. All the women had been attacked with the minimum of a clenched fist, but 59 claimed that kicking was a regular feature. In 42 cases, a weapon was used, usually the first available object, but in fifteen cases this was the same object each time, eight being a belt with a buckle." 87/

This catalogue of injury is not atypical, representing the usual sorts of injury that a battered woman will receive. Thus, studies from Kuwait, 88/ Kenya 89/ and Chile 90/ testify to very similar physical sequelae. Further, physical attack is often accompanied by sexual violence and rape, 91/ the psychological effects of which are perhaps more serious than rape by a stranger given the breach of trust that such conduct involves. 92/

Ultimately, many abused women are murdered by their spouses, study after study revealing that the longer an abused woman remains with her batterer, the greater the odds are that she will be seriously injured. Indeed, instances of battery escalate in frequency and intensity, 93/ research suggesting that where wives are murdered there is usually a long history of physical abuse. 94/ Thus, for example, the New South Wales Bureau of Crime Statistics and Research in Australia indicated that of the homicides cleared up by the police between 1968 and 1981, 42.5 per cent occurred within family relationships, of these 55 per cent of the victims were the spouse and the spouse murdered was usually the woman. 95/ Data from Canada reveal a similar pattern, indicating that during the period 1961-1974, 60 per cent of all female homicide victims were killed within the family context and most often the murderer was the spouse. 96/ Studies from Bangladesh, 97/ Kenya 98/ and Thailand 99/ also serve to verify the fact that murder frequently takes place within the family and most often the victim is a woman.

B.   Short-term effects: health and psychological sequelae for women

Studies examining the emotional and physical health problems of battered women indicate that they report a significantly higher level of anxiety, depression and somatic complaints than women who have not suffered abuse. 100/ Further, often abused women suffer what could be called the "battered woman trauma syndrome", which researchers liken to the "rape trauma syndrome", wherein they exhibit a paralyzing terror that is augmented by the stress of an ever-present threat of attack. 101/ Hilberman and Munson, who studies 60 battered women who were referred to a psychiatric clinic in North Carolina, found the women to be passive, unable to act on their own behalf, fatigued and numb, without energy to do more than minimal household chores or child care. 102/ Such women, further, frequently view themselves as incompetent, unworthy and unlovable and, indeed, deserving of abuse. 103/

Other short-term health implications for battered women are the risk of alcohol and drug abuse, battering having been indicated as a major cause of alcoholism in women. 104/

Battering also increases the risk that the woman will attempt suicide and, perhaps, ultimately succeed. Thus, one study suggests that battered women are 12 times more likely than their non-battered counterparts to attempt suicide, 105/ while evidence from Bangladesh 106/ and India 107/ indicates that victims of abuse within the family frequently find a solution to their problems in suicide.

C.   Short-term effects: effect on the abuser and others

Although wife battery may result in the death of the woman, it can also result in the death of the abuser. A significant amount of research exists which indicates that women who kill their husbands do so in response to an immediate attack or threat of attack from him. 108/ Thus, while wife murder is often the culmination of the pattern of abuse, attacks from the husband may be the reason or motive for his ultimate death.

Wife abuse, moreover, is hazardous for others. Any individual who attempts to intervene runs the risk of injury. Thus, family members may be hurt or killed or may kill the abuser themselves, while evidence from the United States indicates that 33 per cent of all assaults on police officers and 11.5 per cent of police deaths occur in the context of disturbance calls, calls that cover, but are not confined to, domestic disturbances. 109/

D. Effects on children

Many commentators point to the adverse effect violence against a woman may have on her children. In this context, it is important that such effects are noted and taken seriously but, at the same time, it is critical that the needs and concerns of the children of battered women do not become the central or only concern in the debate surrounding domestic violence. Sequelae for children are very serious issues, but should not be used to divert attention from or devalue the problem of the woman.

At its most basic level, children in families where the wife is abused run the real risk that they themselves may be injured or killed by the abuser if they become involved in a battering incident, either by chance or if they attempt to protect their mother. Abusive men will usually assault anybody who dares to challenge their authority. Further, children may, in an attempt to protect their mother, inadvertently kill the abuser. For example, in an incident in Thailand, the 15-year old son of the victim killed his abusive father. 110/

Recent research has suggested that wife assault is one of the major precipitating factors in child abuse, children whose mothers are battered being more than twice as likely than children whose mothers are not battered to be themselves abused, by either their mothers' attacker or their mothers. Stark and Flitcraft, 111/ for example, in their study that compared the records of 600 battered and 600 non-battered women patients, found that child abuse or fear of child abuse existed in 6 per cent of the battered women, while fewer than 1 per cent of the non-battered women appeared to be mothers of abused children. In a further test of a population of abused children and their mothers wherein 116 abused or neglected children were identified, records indicated that 45 per cent of the mothers had been battered, while others had experienced "marital conflict" without direct evidence of deliberate injury. 112/

Apart from physical injury that the child may suffer, it is well established that children from homes where their mothers have been abused suffer significantly more behavioural problems and lack greater social competence than children from homes where there is no wife battery. 113/ Thus, a study by the Metropolitan Police of Bogota, found that 1,299 children had been forced to make the streets their home because of conflicts and marital violence. 114/ Finally, where wife abuse leads to the woman leaving the home and perhaps going to a refuge, children are adversely affected, psychologically, socially and economically. 115/

E. Long-term effects

Frequent assertions are made that violence in the family of origin begets violence 116/ so that children whose mothers were abused by their fathers will go on to repeat that pattern when they themselves establish their families. It is suggested that young men learn to batter their wives from the behaviour of their fathers, while young women learn to become victims of abuse because of the response of their mothers. Again, child abuse is frequently explained as being learned behaviour and thus more prevalent in families where the mother or father had observed or experienced violence in their families of origin (see page 27).

While some studies may go some way to confirm such a hypothesis, it is not without controversy (see page 27), various writers suggesting that no research sample to date supports the conclusion 117/ that a "cycle of violence" exists.

Research does, however, exist which suggests that observation or experience of violence in the family of origin may be implicated in later violent behaviour unconnected with the home. Thus, Jaffe and his colleagues 118/ suggest that boys who grow up in violent homes are likely to have adjustment difficulties and manifest behaviour problems, while Fischer, in a 30-year longitudinal study, discovered that reports on ongoing parental conflict and violence during childhood "... were significantly predictive of serious adult personal crimes (e.g. assault, attempted rape, rape, attempted murder, kidnapping and murder) but were not predictive of serious adult property crimes". 119/

F. Conclusion

Without doubt, wife abuse has important shortand long-term physical, emotional and psychological effects on women, children and men. The personal costs of the problem are thus overwhelming. Furthermore, the social costs of wife battery are enormous, ranging from stigmatization of the individual family and social isolation to temporary or chronic economic dependence of the woman on support groups or the welfare system. The economic costs of the conduct to the community are vast. Estimates suggest that 10 per cent of all victims of family violence in the United States lose work time. 120/ Law enforcement, legal, medical, mental health and other social services are essential in order to protect the woman and attempt to eradicate the behaviour. Thus, again, estimates are that one third of police time in the United States is spent on domestic disturbance calls 121/ and emergency hospital services are over-subscribed by victims of such conduct, 122/ while one Canadian estimate suggests that in 1980 alone, Canadian taxpayers and their governments paid at least thirty-two million Canadian dollars for police intervention in wife battering cases and for related support and administrative services. 123/

Beyond such calculable costs lie the costs in human suffering, which are vast. The most significant long-term effect and ultimate cost of wife battery, however, is the perpetration of the societal structure, confirmed by marital violence, that keeps women inferior and subordinate to men politically, economically and socially.

IV. WHAT CAUSES VIOLENCE AGAINST WOMEN IN THE HOME

Violence against women in the home is thus a widespread problem that has serious consequences for the individual woman, her family and society at large. Responses to the problem are essential, but in order for these responses to be both effective and appropriate it is critical that the cause of the violence should be isolated. Indeed, many attempts have been made to establish the cause of the phenomenon, the search producing a spectrum at the ends of which stand two main theoretical frameworks.

The first, and the earliest, seeks the origins of domestic violence in some form of eradicable cause. It focuses attention on the characteristics of the wife, husband and family, and finds the cause of the violence in the personal inadequacy of the husband or wife or in external stresses that affect the family. Thus, theorists argue that men are violent towards the women with whom they live "because of some internal aberration, abnormality or defective characteristic". 124/ These vary, but include alcoholism, a violent upbringing, mental illness and poor self-control. Others suggest that wives provoke their husbands to beat them or are predisposed to violence, being attracted to violent men and addicted to abuse. Further variations on this analysis based on external causes find the aetiology of wife abuse in stress, frustration and blocked goals, often resulting from unemployment or poverty, which in turn can depend on ethnicity and social class, or on the psychological effects of violent practices or deprived culture.

The second theoretical framework goes beyond an analysis based on psychological or social causes, noting the pervasiveness and acceptability of violence against women in the home and roots its cause in the structure of society itself. It suggests that wife battery is neither a private nor a family problem, but rather a reflection of the broad structures of sexual and economic inequality in society. Indeed, it suggests that violence by husbands against wives is not a breakdown of the social order at all, not an aberration, but rather, "an affirmation of a particular social order", 125/ arising out of the socio-cultural belief that women are less important and less valuable than men and so are not entitled to equal respect. Domestic violence, therefore, is seen as a part of a total social context that tolerates the subordination of women and the use of violence against them as a solution to frustration and conflict. In this analysis, wife abuse is seen as the product of an interrelated and complex set of values wherein women are regarded as inferior to men, suffering discrimination in employment and education and being grossly underrepresented in all areas of social and political life. This inferiority is confirmed particularly within intimate relationships wherein men are assumed to be dominant and women are legally and financially dependant. The analysis further suggests that the subordination of women within relationships and therefore, domestic violence, is condoned by cultural values that emphasize the privacy and autonomy of the family, rendering outside agencies loath to interfere, or if they do so, to stress reconciliation. 126/ This theoretical framework can be best summarized as follows:

"We propose that the correct interpretation of violence between husbands and wives conceptualizes such violence as the extension of the domination and control of husbands over their wives. This control is historically and socially constructed. The beginning of an adequate analysis of violence between husbands and wives is the consideration of the history of the family, of the status of women therein and of violence directed against them. This analysis will substantiate our claim that violence in the family should be understood primarily as coercive control." 127/

While other theories have been advanced to explain domestic violence, most locate themselves along this broad spectrum. The following thus attempts to survey the literature that has analysed the causes of violence against wives, starting first with those explanations that find the causes in external factors.

A. Alcohol and drugs

Research has shown that there is a close relationship between the consumption of alcohol and drugs and violence in the home, such substances playing as significant a role in the instigation of domestic violence as they do in violence in other contexts. Thus, Hilberman's study of 60 battered women in a general medical clinic revealed that drinking accompanied 93 per cent of the incidents, 128/ while Renvoize indicated that alcohol was a factor in 40 per cent of the cases she investigated. 129/ Similarly, Gelles discovered, in his 1974 study of violence in families in New Hampshire, that drinking accompanied violence in 48 per cent of the families where assaults had occurred. 130/ Indeed, many of the women in his sample revealed that their husbands only hit them when they were drunk. Further evidence supporting the link between alcohol and assaults against wives can be found in Gayford's study, where 52 per cent of his sample of women who had been abused stated that their husbands were drunk at least once a week, while another 22 per cent indicated that the violence only occurred when the man was under the influence of alcohol, 131/ Scott's study of the wives of 100 alcoholics, 132/ Pahl's study of 42 women who had used a women's refuge in the United Kingdom 133/ and evidence gleaned from surveys in Australia. 134/ Studies from Poland indicate that the one cause of violence against wives is alcoholism and that this is endemic in the country. 135/

Although research into the subject is very new in developing countries, similar findings have been made in Papua New Guinea, 136/ Samoa, 137/ Uganda, 138/ Chile, 139/ Kuwait 140/ and Colombia. 141/

It is clear that there is an association between alcohol use and violence against wives, but the precise role of alcohol in the domestic context has yet to be determined. It has been suggested that re-analysis of studies that stress the link between wife abuse and alcohol may reveal that the relationship is meaningless as very little distinction is made in such studies between alcoholism or pathological drinking and episodic drinking associated with violence. 142/ Moreover, while the studies that do exist reveal that many abusive husbands are heavy drinkers, many of the men who beat their wives when they are drunk, also beat them when they are sober. 143/ Further, drunkenness exists in many families that are non-violent and violence is present in others where there is no alcohol abuse. 144/

The studies suggest that in cases where violence is associated with alcohol, the link is peculiarly male as wives rarely become violent towards their husbands and children when inebriated. 145/ Some evidence also exists that links male drunkenness, ultimately resulting in an assault on the wife, with male drinking parties, during which men give each other support and encouragement and reaffirm their role as breadwinner and boss. 146/

Drunkenness, therefore, is perhaps best seen not as a "cause" of violence, but as a condition that coexists with it. Indeed, men who wish to carry out a violent act may become drunk in order to perform the act. After the violence has occurred, both the man and his wife may excuse his behaviour on the ground that he was drunk and therefore not responsible for his actions. In the end analysis, all that the studies which put forward the view that there is a connection between alcohol or drug abuse and wife beating indicate is that men who are drunk or drugged do beat their wives. They do not show us that they beat them because they are under the influence of alcohol or drugs. It may well be that they drink or take drugs in order to justify beating their wives.

B. Cycle of violence: violence as learned behaviour

A number of researchers locate the origins of wife assault in the childhood of the abusive man, suggesting that the violence occurs because he has witnessed or experienced violence in his family of origin. Thus, Straus, Steinmetz and Gelles 147/ concluded from their survey of intact couples in the United States that "the majority of today's violent couples are those who were brought up by parents who were violent to each other" 148/ and that there is a "clear trend for violence in childhood to produce violence in adult life ... violence by parents begets violence in the next generation". 149/ They reported that compared to men from non-violent families of origin, men who saw their parents attack each other were 3 times as likely to hit their wives and 10 times more likely to attack them with a weapon. Even if they had only witnessed "wife beating" - hitting without punching or weapons - they were more likely to be violent adults, only 2 per cent of men from non-violent homes hitting their wives, while 20 per cent of men from the "most violent" families did so. Moreover, among 13 per cent of their sample who reported being hit as teenagers, fully 35 per cent indicated that they hit their wives, as opposed to only 11 per cent of those who were not so hit.

Similar conclusions were reached by Stacey and Shupe 150/ who determined from their research sample that 6 out of 10 abusive men had witnessed physical violence between their parents, 4 out of 10 had been neglected by their parents and 4 out of 10 had been abused by their parents. They found, further, that 1 out of 3 of the batterers' brothers and sisters had been abused by their parents and in two thirds of the childhood homes where the batterers had been abused their siblings had been also. 151/

The theory that violence is learned behaviour and is cyclical is a popular one and has tended to be perpetuated by folk wisdom and personal impressions. A number of writers have, however, questioned its validity, particularly attacking the studies that are presented to support it.

It is suggested that many of the publications widely cited to support the theory present no empirical data, 152/ often relying on self-reports from small criminal subgroups, anecdotal information from battered women on their husbands, individual case histories and reports from service providers. 153/ Of those that produce data, a number draw on samples that are small and unrepresentative, frequently being based on groups of people known either to be violent in some way, or to be the victims of violence, whose backgrounds are then examined for evidence of violence in their families of origin. 154/ Further, even those studies that draw on a wide data base are problematic. No consistent definition of violence is used, rendering such studies inappropriate for comparative research, and most definitions used are ambiguous. 155/ If, as Dobash and Dobash point out, the definition is sufficiently vague, almost everyone will come from a violent family. Thus, information that a mass murderer was sometimes slapped as a child will lend support to the cycle of violence theory, but will hardly be concrete confirmation. 156/ Moreover, it is rare to find studies that are designed to include comparisons or controls. Little attention has been paid, for example, to the siblings of the individuals studied, so it is often unknown whether they too have violent families. Results, therefore, which indicate that one in three husbands who are abusive were themselves abused will suggest that the cycle of violence thesis is accurate, but at the same time will cast doubt on the analysis as two out of three, or the majority, of such husbands come from non-violent homes. 157/

It seems, thus, that while there is support for the theory that violence is cyclical, much more sophisticated research, which compares violent and non-violent individuals from violent and non-violent homes, is required to test it. Certainly, it is wrong to assume that all children of men who abuse their wives or all men that have themselves been abused will abuse their wives. The most that can be said is that a violent family of origin is yet another variable that may be involved in the aetiology of violence against wives.

C. Victim precipitation

Suggestions have been made that wife battery is caused by the behaviour or personality of the victim. Hence, some researchers believe that violence arises when the victim reduces her husband's self-control by verbally tormenting him until he is no longer in control of his responses. 158/ Others conclude that women have a psychological need for domination, excitement and attention, 159/ one theory going so far as to hypothesize that women become addicted to the excitement and stimulation brought about by the violence because of some form of chemical reaction. 160/

Research indicates that while patterns of this nature may exist, they are not the norm. Often a man will abuse a woman without any warning, let alone provocation, sometimes waking her from sleep to do so. Further, there is evidence which indicates that women do not seek out successive abusive relationships, which casts doubt on these psychological theories. Pahl's study, for example, of 42 women who had used a refuge in the United Kingdom, revealed that not one of the women who went on to another relationship was abused in that partnership; however, their abusers went on to replicate the pattern of abuse in their new relationships. 161/

As Dobash and Dobash observe, moreover, the types of behaviour defined by researchers and husbands as provocative are diverse, ranging from aggression, nagging and emasculation to submission. Thus, they point out:

"Being too talkative or too quiet, too sexual or not sexual enough, too frugal or too extravagant, too often pregnant or not frequently enough all seem to be provocative. The only pattern discernible in these lists is that the behaviour, whatever it might be, represents some form of failure or refusal on the part of the woman to comply with or support her husband's wishes and authority." 162/

They point out, also, and this must be stressed, that explanations of wife abuse that rely on victim precipitation are dangerous. Such explanations accept the use of violence and also perpetuate the stereotype of female submission in intimate relationships. 163/ As such, they absolve the man of his responsibility and place blame for the abuse on the woman.

D. Mental illness

Some theorists have characterized men who are violent in the home as passive, indecisive and sexually inadequate. Their wives, by contrast, are seen as aggressive, masculine and masochistic. Others see men who abuse their wives as psychopaths. 164/ While some violent men are indeed sick, the widespread incidence of domestic violence against women and the variety of personality types, both women and men, who are involved in it, suggests that this is not a common cause of the conduct.

E. Stress, frustration, role frustration

Early scholarship on violence against wives emphasized the role of stress in its aetiology. Thus, the British Association of Social Workers stated:

> "Economic conditions, low wages, bad housing, overcrowding and
> isolation: unfavourable and frustrating work conditions for the man:
> lack of job opportunities for adolescents/school-leavers and lack of
> facilities such as day care (e.g. nurseries), adequate transport,
> pleasant environment and play space and recreational facilities, for
> mother and children were considered to cause personal desperation
> that might precipitate violence in the home." 165/

Explanations indicating stress as the cause of domestic violence, at the outset, directed attention to stresses derived from economic and social disadvantage. As such violence against wives was seen as a primarily lower class phenomenon as this class was most susceptible to such pressures. Again, however, while it is possible for economic and social stresses to incite violence, theorists who rely on stress as the explanation for such violence are unable to explain why all men subject to such pressure do not abuse their wives.

F. Underdevelopment

Research into family violence is very new in developing countries. A number of scholars have, however, addressed the issue and see family violence as a particular by-product of underdevelopment. Thus, research from Chile points to the subsistence existence and economic dependence of many families involved in domestic abuse, 166/ Nigeria, to the economic crisis of many such families, 167/ Kenya, 168/ to the gaps between the rich and the poor, the urban and the rural and the powerful and powerless, and Egypt 169/ and Bangladesh 170/ to tensions in society. It is suggested that in situations of underdevelopment violence becomes inherent as the result of a system wherein there is political and economic deprivation and oppression of individuals leading to social injustice. 170/ In many developing countries, traditional social norms and practices, which may have once served to restrain wife abuse, are in the process of disintegration, 168/ populations in the cities have swollen as migration from the rural areas has taken place as people have sought individual economic opportunities, and basic resources and services have proved to be inadequate. In such societies, poor housing and a precarious economic existence appear inevitable and violence becomes almost a way of life. 168/ Such violence is vented against the most powerless who are inevitably women. 169/

This theory, which is a variation on the theme that stress and frustration produce wife abuse, may well have some validity. Again, however, it fails to explain why all men in deprived circumstances are not violent to their wives and why many men in economically privileged positions in both industrialized societies and developing countries are violent to their wives.

G. Cultural factors

In a number of societies customs or beliefs are offered to explain the existence of wife abuse. Thus, it is common for African surveys to indicate that wife abuse occurs because beating shows that the man loves the woman, that this is expected by her and that she will feel rejected if she is not beaten. 171/ Similarly, it is suggested that wives need beating. 168/

South Asian studies point to the custom of dowry as a precipitating factor in wife abuse. Dowry is an important part of the negotiations for an arranged marriage, parents accepting that if they wish their daughters to be married, they must provide a suitable dowry. Recently, the custom has combined with the growth in consumerism and has become, in some cases, a life and death matter for the bride. This is because her husband or his family may consider the dowry that has been provided to be inadequate and harass the woman, sometimes to the point of death by murder or suicide, in order to extract more from her natal family. 172/

Again, while certainly such customs may be factors in wife abuse, they do not explain why only some husbands in such systems abuse their wives.

H. Structural inequality: the position of women in the family and society

The overwhelming pervasiveness of violence against wives in the family led scholars to question the validity of explanations for the phenomenon that were based on an external cause. Further, studies that sought such causal explanations had discovered some "causes" for such violence that when taken together led inevitably to a new analysis.

For example, some researchers concluded that violence occurred when men failed to live up to the traditional stereotype of male superiority. Such could occur if the man believed he was an under-achiever in employment or education, 173/ if he were denied access to power and prestige outside the home 174/ or if his wife were perceived to be a superior achiever. 175/ Others pointed to jealousy, 176/ disputes over money 177/ and the wife's right to personal autonomy. 178/ Surveys of women who were abused revealed that their husbands liked to dominate financial management within the family, 179/ often keeping them chronically short of money and even forcing them to give them their wages or, if available, their government benefit. 180/ Other surveys indicated that very often the abuser was unemployed. 181/

Treated separately, such indications would result in a "cause"-based analysis, but looked at in aggregate they revealed a common thread, such being that there was an assumption by the man that he should be the dominant party in a relationship that was traditionally unequal and that where such dominance was threatened by some factor, even the woman's separateness as a human being, dominance would be reasserted, if necessary, by violence. 182/

This common thread opened the way to an analysis that found the origins of violence against women in the family in the structure of the family itself, a structure that is mirrored and confirmed in the structure of society, which condones the oppression of women and tolerates male violence as one of the instruments in the perpetuation of this power balance. Hence, Straus concluded 183/ "... wife beating is not just a personal abnormality, but rather it has its roots in the very structuring of society and the family; that in the cultural norms and in the sexist organization of society".

This analysis has been taken even further by scholars, primarily feminists, who suggest that wife abuse is typical, not rare behaviour and, indeed, behaviour consistent with and condoned by general attitudes. They stress that economic, social and political factors are all interconnected, creating a structure wherein the low economic position of women is linked with their vulnerability to violence within the household. This, in turn, is connected to their powerlessness in relation to the State and men in general, 184/ thereby resulting in a tacit acceptance by the community of abusive conduct within the home. This acceptance becomes manifest in societal attitudes that allow husbands to view their wives as chattels and that stress the privacy and autonomy of the family. 185/

The analysis of wife abuse as a structural rather than a causal phenomenon began in the industrialized West. However, studies from developing countries have served to confirm rather than cast doubt on its validity. Thus, studies from India 186/ suggest that family violence may be a by-product of the societal structure where authority lies in the male with the female conditioned to accept her secondary role. A Chinese study similarly finds the root of such behaviour in the male-centred ideology in China where a husband will abuse his wife where something is not done to his satisfaction, even, for example, if the wife gives birth to a girl. 187/ Confirmation is found in other studies from developing countries which reveal that violence often occurs when the man wishes to take another wife, 188/ where he suspects his wife of infidelity 189/ and where he sees his wife as "rebellious", because of her ascending liberation 190/ or because of her "nagging". 191/

This analysis, which goes beyond the search for an external cause and locates the origin of violence against women in the family in the structure of marriage and the family and in the wider society, in sum, argues that it is impossible to understand the nature of wife assault without taking account of the social and ideological context within which it occurs. 192/ The analysis leads us to question the family as an institution and also leads us to question the role of society, particularly the helping professions, such as the police, the courts, the medical profession, in the tacit condonation of a structure that "supports the male's use of violence to maintain his dominance over his mate". 193/

I. Conclusion

Explanations of violence against women move, therefore, from explanations that seek the origin of the abuse in an individualized cause to an approach that sees the issue as located in a broader social-structural context, focusing upon the entire social situation within which the violence takes place. This approach stresses the subordination of women within society that allows them to become the "appropriate" 194/ victims of marital violence.

While this analysis is helpful, the fact remains that although violence against women in the family is common it is not universal, thus explanations of such violence must go beyond a mere assertion that violence against women arises out of structural inequality and will exist as long as men are regarded as more important than women. Certainly, such inequality is the context in which such violence is condoned and even encouraged and the context in which violence against women in the home becomes crystallized as a cultural and societal norm. Notwithstanding this, the analysis fails to explain how sociological and cultural factors that are universal, interact with individual personal behaviour. 195/

One commentator has attempted to grapple with this difficulty and while basing her analysis in the theory that domestic violence arises out of a social structure that perpetuates the subjugation of women as a community to the overall dominance of men as a community, she suggests that there are three particular situations wherein the social and cultural norm will result in violence against the wife. 196/ Thus, she hypothesizes that wife assault is most likely to occur in three "milieus", a term she uses to encompass the norms, values and attitudes of a particular cultural context, the traditional, transitional and modern industrial.

In the traditional milieu, where social norms and customary law tolerate some use of physical force as a means of disciplining female members of the family in certain circumstances, the man is usually afforded a right to sanction what is regarded as unsuitable behaviour, the sanctionable behaviour being primarily sexual and being regarded as involving the man's honour. Here, clearly, violence against the wife will arise out of her subordination, but if the man who perpetrates the violence is traditionally assigned authority over her, such violence will be considered legitimate, and, indeed, not even defined as violence. If, however, a man who has not been granted authority over her performs the same act, as the purpose of the violence is not in accordance with tradition, sanctions may be available.

Migrant populations, refugees and others in situations where the modes of living and authority structures are in transition and flux come within the definition of the transitional milieu. Here, attitudes, mores and roles are changing rapidly and frequently the male's position is threatened, as often he is no longer in a position to support the family, and the woman may be obliged to undertake tasks and responsibilities that challenge previously held beliefs and attitudes. In this context, the man may seek to establish his dominance within the relationship by means of force. 197/

The third situation wherein domestic violence is common is the modern, industrial milieu. Here the official ideology proclaims the equality of the sexes, permitting neither the expression of male authority over women, nor any coercive measures to maintain such authority. In this milieu, however, there is a gap between prevalent attitudes and the law, the legal system being characterized by unevenness and contradictions. Hence, while the expressed philosophy is that violence against women in the family is unacceptable, the law may still tacitly condone such violence by, for example, not criminalizing marital rape.

The approach outlined above confirms and extends the analysis of violence against women in the domestic context as arising out of a power structure where men are traditionally dominant within the family and society. Other analyses that similarly accept this structural background suggest that violence erupts because of the general acceptance of violence as a reasonable response to frustration, conflict or despair, such acceptance being manifested in the existence of war, sport, the encouragement of violence in various subcultures, and its popularity and celebration in the media. 198/

The combination of structural inequality within the family and society and the general acceptability of violence as a method of conflict resolution within society as the fundamental cause of violence against wives is attractive, appearing to be a rational and logical explanation. However, there is no empirical data to support it as there have been no studies that have compared the level of violence against wives in societies at war with societies at peace, the level of violence against wives in societies with violent punishments with those without them and societies with standing armies with those without. Finally, there is little empirical data linking violence in the media with violence in the home. 199/

In sum, it would appear that there is no simple explanation for violence against women in the home. Certainly, any explanation must go beyond the individual characteristics of the man, the woman and the family and look to the structure of relationships and the role of society in underpinning that structure. In the end analysis, it is perhaps best to conclude that violence against wives is a function of the belief, fostered in all cultures, that men are superior and that the women they live with are their possessions or chattels that they can treat as they wish and as they consider appropriate.

In some societies, this philosophy is reinforced by devices such as bride price 200/ that lead a man to believe that he has bought his wife and thus his conduct towards her should not be open to question. Even in those societies where there are no such overt indications of subordination, the social framework relegates the woman, none the less, to the level of a chattel. Here structures place her in a position of dependence on the man and predict that she will fulfil certain roles. This combines with the isolation of the family as an institution and the respect that is offered to it in terms of privacy and autonomy by all agents within the society, to allow violence to occur if the wife is seen to overstep her traditional role.

The collected scholarship that seeks to explain violence against women in the home indicates that the explanation is complex and certainly multi-factorial. Any explanation must, however, be seen against a background of gender inequality, wherein the victim of such violence is most often the woman and the perpetrator most often the man and wherein the structures of society − be they economic, political or legal − act to confirm this inequality.

Notes

1/ See, Davidson, "Wife beating a recurring problem throughout history", in Battered Women: A Psychosociological Study of Domestic Violence, M. Roy, ed. (London, Van Nostrand Reinhold, 1977); R. E. Dobash and R. Dobash, Violence Against Wives: A Case Against the Patriarchy (London, Open Books, 1980), pp. 31-75.

2/ Consider, for example, such adages as: "A dog, a wife and a walnut tree, the more you beat them the better they be". Further, symbolic beating of the woman on her wedding night by her husband is a part of some tribal wedding rituals.

3/ W. Blackstone, Commentaries on the Laws of England (1775); see also, J. C. Jeaffreson, Brides and Bridals (London, 1872) who maintained that it was possible to thrash a woman with a cudgel, but not knock her down with an iron bar.

4/ Bradley v. State 2 Miss 156 (1824), p. 158: a man was legally permitted to chastise his wife "without subjecting himself to vexatious prosecutions for assault and battery, resulting in the mutual discredit and shame of all parties concerned". See also, State v. Black 60 N.C 162, 86 Am. Dec. 436 (1864). The English common law right of a husband to physically chastise his wife was abolished in R v. Jackson (1890) 1 A.B 671.

5/ S. Edwards, "Male violence against women: excusatory and explanatory ideologies in law and society", in her Gender, Sex and the Law (London, Croom Helm, 1985), p. 188; E. Pleck, "Feminist responses to 'crimes against women', 1858-1896", Signs, No. 8, 1983, p. 451.

6/ Edwards, loc cit., pp. 189-191.

7/ Ibid. Murder charges, for example, were frequently reduced to manslaughter.

8/ K. Waits, "The criminal justice system's response to battering: understanding the problem, forging the solutions", Washington Law Review, No. 60, 1985, p. 268.

9/ Edwards, loc. cit., pp. 191-192.

10/ J. S. Mill, The Subjection of Women (London, Virago Edition, 1983), p. 57.

11/ Ibid., see his further remarks on pp. 25-26 and 63.

12/ Frances Power Cobbe, "Wife torture in England", Contemporary Review, April 1878; Pleck, loc. cit., p. 452; Dobash and Dobash, op. cit., pp. 64-74.

13/ The British activist Erin Pizzey is credited with first bringing the problem to public attention in 1971 when she opened the first women's shelter. See, E. Pizzey, Scream Quietly or the Neighbours Will Hear (London, Penguin, 1974).

14/ In the United States the campaign dates from 1975 with the establishment of a Task Force on Battered Women and Household Violence by the National Organisation for Women.

15/ Campaigns were established in Australia, Canada, New Zealand. The shelter system appears now to be almost world wide.

16/ The case study from Kenya indicates that women are at risk from all their male relatives (B. N. Wamalwa, Nairobi, Public Law Institute, 1987).

17/ M. D. Freeman, "Doing his best to sustain the sanctity of marriage", in Marital Violence, N. Johnson, ed., Sociological Review Monograph No. 31 (London, Routledge and Kegan Paul, 1985), p. 124; P. Bart, "Rape does not end with a kiss", Viva, June 1975; I. H. Frieze, "Investigating the causes and consequences of marital rape", Signs, No. 8, 1983, p. 532.

18/ R. Gelles, The Violent Home (Beverly Hills, Sage, 1972), p. 145: 10 out of 44 women he interviewed reported being beaten when pregnant. S. K. Steinmetz, The Cycle of Violence: Assertive, Aggressive and Abusive Family Interaction (New York, Praeger, 1977), p. 77, indicates that pregnancy is a major inducement to violence, a suggestion supported by J. J. Gayford, "Battered wives" in Violence and the Family, J. P. Martin, ed. (New York, John Wiley, 1978), p. 21.

19/ R. E. Dobash and R. Dobash, "Wives: the "appropriate" victims of marital violence?", Victimology, No. 2, 1978, p. 426. M. D. Pagelow, "The battered husband syndrome: social problem or much ado about little?", in Marital Violence, N. Johnson, ed., Sociological Review Monograph 31 (London, Routledge and Kegan Paul, 1985), p. 172.

20/   J. Scutt, <u>Even in the Best of Homes: Violence in the Family</u> (Sidney, Penguin, 1982), chap. 4; D. Finkelhor, <u>Sexually Victimised Children</u> (New York, Free Press, 1979), p. 88, estimates man-girl incest to involve 1% of girls. See also, J. Herman and L. Hirschman, "Father-daughter incest", <u>Signs</u>, No. 2, 1977, p. 742, who estimate the figure to be higher. See further, D. Finkelhor, <u>A Sourcebook on Child Sexual Abuse</u> (Beverly Hills, Sage, 1986), which in chapter one provides a survey of Canadian and United States surveys of child sexual abuse, all of which reveal that female children are the most common victims of such assault and their most common molesters men, frequently fathers or father substitutes.

21/   N. P. Simi, case study from Samoa (Prime Minister's Department, Apia); and K. N. Pryce, case study from Trinidad and Tobago (St. Augustine, University of the West Indies).

22/   See, for example, Report of the New South Wales Domestic Violence Committee, which reported that a radio talk back show in Sydney revealed that four out of the ten callers were mothers who had been battered by their sons (New South Wales Government, Women's Co-ordination Unit, 9 September 1985), p. 53.

23/   The literature documenting child abuse and child neglect is vast, beginning from the 1961 presentation by C. Henry Kempe to the Annual Meeting of the American Academy of Pediatrics entitled "The battered child syndrome". The literature has emerged from most countries and cultures, but North American, European and Australian research predominates.

24/   L.E.M. Mukasa-Kikonyogo, Ugandan case study (Kampala, High Court of Uganda, 1987).

25/   See, for example, violence related to dowry where very often the husband's female relatives are violent towards the women. See, L. Akanda and I. Shamim, "Women and violence: a comparative study of rural and urban violence in Bangladesh", <u>Women's Issue</u> (Dhaka), No. 1, November 1984; J. Huq, "Status of women in Bangladesh", in <u>Women and the Law</u>; F.R.P. Romero, ed. (U.P. Law Centre), pp. 37-38; U. Sharma, "Dowry in North India: its consequences for women", in R. Hirschon, <u>Women and Property - Women as Property</u> (London, Croom Helm, 1984), p. 62; and I. Shamim, case study from Bangladesh (Dhaka, Department of Sociology, University of Dhaka).

26/   Mukasa-Kikonyogo, <u>op. cit.</u>

27/   See, for example, M. Straus, R. J. Gelles and Steinmetz, <u>Behind Closed Doors: Violence in the American Family</u> (New York, Anchor Books, 1980); Gelles, <u>op. cit</u>.

28/   S. K. Steinmetz, "Wife beating, husband beating - a comparison of the use of physical violence between spouses to resolve marital fights", in <u>Battered Women</u>, M. Roy, ed. (New York, Von Nostrand Reinhold, 1977), p. 63; S. K. Steinmetz, "The battered husband syndrome", <u>Victimology</u>, No. 2, 1978, p. 499; S. K. Steinmetz, "Women and violence: victims and perpetrators", <u>American Journal of Psychotherapy</u>, No. 34, 1980, p. 334.

29/   "The battered husband syndrome", <u>Time Magazine</u>, 20 March 1978, p. 69.

30/   Figures moved from 250,000 husbands per year to 12 million husbands per year. Pagelow, <u>loc. cit.</u>, p. 173.

31/ M. D. Fields and R. M. Kirchner, "Battered women are still in need: a reply to Steinmetz", <u>Victimology</u>, No. 3, 1978, p. 216, indicated that Steinmetz's essay on violent wives had been used to defeat efforts to obtain funding for a shelter for battered women in Chicago.

32/ Dobash and Dobash, "Wives: the appropriate victims ..."; Fields and Kirchner, <u>loc. cit.</u>; E. Pleck and others, "The battered data syndrome: a comment on Steinmetz's article", <u>Victimology</u>, No. 2, 1978, p. 680. These authors claim that Steinmetz misrepresented her data, a claim supported by Pagelow, who concludes "In sum, the data Steinmetz provided simply do not agree with her claim that "not only the percentage of wives having used physical violence often exceed that of the husbands, but that wives also exceed husbands in the frequency with which these acts occur"" (Pagelow, <u>loc. cit.</u>, p. 176). See also, D. J. Bell, "Domestic violence: victimisation, police intervention and disposition", <u>Journal of Criminal Justice</u>, No. 13, 1985, p. 425.

33/ <u>Ibid.</u>, and see Pagelow, <u>loc. cit.</u>, p. 172; M. H. Mitchell, "Does wife abuse justify homicide?", <u>Wayne Law Review</u>, No. 24, 1978, p. 1705; N. Wolfe, "Victim provocation: the battered wife and legal definition of self defense", <u>Sociological Symposium</u>, No. 25, 1979, p. 98.

34/ See notes 17 and 18; and Straus, Gelles and Steinmetz, <u>op. cit.</u>, p. 43.

35/ W. Stojanowska, case study from Poland (Warsaw, Instytut Badania Prawa Sadowego, 1987).

36/ S. Skrobanek, case study from Thailand (Bangkok, Women's Information Centre, 1987).

37/ M. Straus, "Wife beating: how common and why?", <u>Victimology</u>, No. 2, 1978, p. 443; Note here the comment of W. Brienes and L. Gordon, "The new scholarship on family violence", <u>Signs</u>, No. 8, 1983, p. 510, who suggest that the controversy over "husband beating" arose out of the fact that Straus, Steinmetz and Gelles condemned every act of violence and failed to trace the origin of the violence which had been perpetrated by the woman. They note that most of Steinmetz's critics attacked her data and her extrapolations therefrom. They, on the other hand, criticize her total condemnation of violence which renders a woman who resorts to such uncharacteristic behaviour, for example, self defence, as culpable and less deserving of sympathy than a woman who is totally passive.

38/ M. Straus and R. J. Gelles, "Societal change in family violence from 1975 to 1985 as revealed by two national surveys", <u>Journal of Marriage and the Family</u>, No. 48, 1986, pp. 465, 471.

39/ M. Borkowski, M. Murch and V. Walker, <u>Marital Violence: The Community Response</u> (London, Tavistock 1983), p. 11.

40/ See, for example, Borkowski, Murch and Walker, <u>op. cit.</u>; J. Pahl, ed., <u>Private Violence and Public Policy: The Needs of Battered Women and the Response of the Social Services</u> (London, Routledge and Kegan Paul, 1985); R. J. Gelles, <u>The Violent Home ...</u>; R. J. Gelles, <u>Family Violence</u> (Beverly Hills, Sage, 1979); Pizzey, <u>op. cit.</u>; Scutt, <u>op. cit.</u>; L. MacLeod, <u>Wife Battering in Canada: The Vicious Circle</u> (Ottawa, Canadian Advisory Council on the Status of Women, 1980); Attorney-General's Task Force on Family Violence, Final Report (Washington, D.C., September 1984).

41/ See case studies, for example, which represent indications that 24
United Nations countries have problems with violence against women in the home.
Further, the Women and Development Programme of the Commonwealth Secretariat
administered a questionnaire to all Commonwealth countries in 1984 and specifically asked whether domestic violence was a problem in the country. All
respondents indicated that the problem existed.

42/ D. Marsden, "Sociological perspectives on family violence", in
Violence and the Family, J. Martin, ed. (Chichester, Wiley, 1978); see, also
Gelles' research: see note 40 and Mukasa-Kikonyogo, op. cit., wherein a
questionnaire survey was taken which revealed that most of the victims and
abusers were what could be termed lower class or were from the rural areas.
See, further, the studies undertaken by the Papua New Guinea Law Reform Commission, Domestic Violence in Rural Papua New Guinea, Occasional Paper No. 18
(Boroko, 1985); Domestic Violence in Urban Papua New Guinea, Occasional Paper
No. 19 (Boroko, 1986) which revealed that domestic violence was more common in
the lower and rural classes. However, note the results of a study by the
British Medical Research Council which carried out three years of intensive
interviews with a random group of 286 women, not then in refuges. This study
reveals that 57% of the middle class women in the sample - admittedly only 59
of the group - had suffered violence, while 51% of the working class women had
done so. B. Andrews and G. W. Brown, "Marital violence in the community: a
biographical approach", British Journal of Psychiatry, vol. 153, 1988, p. 305.

43/ See, for example, E. Stark, A. Flitcraft and W. Frazier, "Medicine
and the patriarchy: the social construction of a private event", International
Journal of Health Services, No. 9, 1979, p. 461; Straus, Gelles and Steinmetz,
op. cit., pp. 123-152.

44/ No comprehensive research has been undertaken in Nigeria into the
problem. However, the case study by J. O. Akande, reveals that police
sometimes received complaints from women who tend to come from poor and
polygamous homes and the Social Welfare department does have such cases on
file. Professor Akande who wrote the case study did an informal study amongst
educated women and found that they too were susceptible to abuse (Lagos,
Faculty of Law, Lagos State University).

45/ See notes 42 and 43; see also Borkowski, Murch and Walker, op. cit.,
p. 31; Pahl, op. cit.; P. Montgomery and V. Bell, Police Response to Wife
Assault: A Northern Ireland Study (Northern Ireland Women's Aid Federation,
1986), p. 21; B. A. Al-Awadi, Kuwaiti case study (Safat, University of
Kuwait); Simi, op. cit.; MacLeod, Battered But not Beaten ..., p. 21.

46/ Ibid; Pahl, op. cit., and notes 40 and 42.

47/ See U.S. Attorney-General's Task Force on Family Violence, Final
Report (September 1984) and L. H. Herrington, case study on the United States,
p. 5; see also, K. Waits, "The criminal justice system's response to battering:
understanding the problem, forging the solutions", Washington Law Review,
No. 60, 1985, pp. 276-277, for examples of "upper class" battering.

48/ I. Shamim, case study from Bangladesh (Dhaka, University of Dhaka,
Department of Sociology, 1987).

49/ All studies appear to suggest that this is the case, see notes 42,
43, 44 and 45.

50/ R. E. Dobash, "When non-sexist language is sexist", in Battered Women's Director, B. Warrior, ed., ninth edition (Richmond, Earlham College, 1985), p. 198.

51/ Pahl, op. cit., p. 5.

52/ E. Wilson, The Existing Research into Battered Women (London, National Women's Aid Federation, 1976), pp. 5-6.

53/ S. Toft, ed., Domestic Violence in Papua New Guinea, Monograph No. 3 (Boroko, Papua New Guinea Law Reform Commission, 1986); Law Reform Commission, Domestic Violence in Rural Papua New Guinea ...; Law Reform Commission, Domestic Violence in Urban Papua New Guinea ....

54/ Case studies: Nigeria: J. O. Akande reviewed Social Service files and conducted informal interviews; Colombia: A. M. Berenguer surveyed 1,170 bodily injury cases, see also p. 8 of the study which suggests that violence in the family is common in Colombia affecting the vast majority; Bangladesh: case study reveals that research so far has been confined to murder and dowry related violence; Chile: case study authors themselves carried out retrospective analysis of hospital files. See also Ugandan case study where a small survey was taken; Kuwaiti case study, where a survey was taken and the studies from Thailand and Kenya where newspaper reports were surveyed.

55/ See Part Two, chap. II.

56/ Dobash and Dobash, Violence Against Wives ..., p. 15.

57/ Criminal Statistics, 1982, England and Wales, Cmnd. 9048 (London, HM Stationery Office), table 4.4; E. Gibson and S. Klein, Murder (1957-1968), Home Office Research Study No. 3 (London, HM Stationery Office, 1969).

58/ H. von Hentig, The Criminal and His Victim (New Haven, Connecticut, Shoe String, 1948).

59/ M. E. Wolfgang, Patterns in Criminal Homicide (Philadelphia, University of Pennsylvania, 1958). See also, California Commission on the Status of Women, Domestic Violence Fact Sheet (Sacramento, California, 1978), and the United States President's Commission on Law Enforcement and the Administration of Justice, Task Force Report, Crime and Its Impact - An Assessment (Washington, D.C., Government Printing Office, 1967), p. 15, which states that the risk of serious attack from spouses, family members, friends and acquaintances is nearly twice as great as that from strangers.

60/ Shamim, op. cit.

61/ British Crime Survey, First Report, Home Office Research Study, No. 76 (London, HM Stationery Office, 1982).

62/ Criminal Statistics, England and Wales, 1980, Cmnd. 8376 (London, HM Stationery Office), table 2.5.

63/ R. E. Dobash, and R. Dobash, Violence Against Wives in Scotland (Scottish Home and Health Department, 1979). See also, F. H. McClintock, Crimes of Violence (London, Macmillan, 1963), who indicates that in 27% of crimes known to the police the offender and victim are related by marriage.

64/ Stojanowska, op. cit.

65/ Vanuatu National Council of Women, Comments on the Proposed Family Law Bill, May 1985, para. 36.

66/ M. I. Plata, case study from Colombia (Bogota, Population Concern, 1987); ISIS Internacional, case study from Chile (Santiago, 1987).

67/ Borkowski, Murch and Walker, op. cit., pp. 26-27; R. Chester and J. Streather, "Cruelty in English divorce: some empirical findings", Journal of Marriage and the Family, No. 34, 1972, p. 706.

68/ MacLeod, Wife Battering in Canada ..., p. 20.

69/ G. Levinger, "Sources of marital dissatisfaction among applicants for divorce", American Journal of Orthopsychiatry, No. 36, 1966, p. 803.

70/ M. El Husseiny Zaalouk, case study from Egypt (Cairo, National Center for Social and Criminal Research, 1987).

71/ C. D. Spinellis, case study from Greece (Athens, University of Athens, Faculty of Law, 1987).

72/ Pryce, op. cit.

73/ Report of the Working Party of the London Metropolitan Police, London, U.K., 1986, unpublished, projected on the basis of the numbers of such orders awarded at a small court district in London that 6,000 such orders would be awarded throughout the city each year.

74/ Pahl, op. cit., p. 76.

75/ MacLeod, Wife Battering in Canada ..., p. 16; L. MacLeod, Battered But Not Beaten (Ottawa, Advisory Council on the Status of Women, 1987), pp. 6-7, indicates that in 1985, 110 transition houses in Canada accommodated 20,291 women, 15,730 who were admitted because they had been abused by their partner.

76/ See, for example, Malaysia, where there are two women's refuges. S. Papachan, case study from Malaysia (Selangor, Women's Aid Organisation, 1987).

77/ Straus, Gelles and Steinmetz, op. cit. Similar results were retrieved from a telephone survey undertaken in Kentucky in 1981. M. Schulman, A Survey of Spousal Abuse Against Women in Kentucky (New York, Louis Harris, 1979).

78/ M. Straus and R. J. Gelles, "Societal change in family violence from 1975 to 1985 as revealed by two national surveys", Journal of Marriage and the Family, No. 48, 1986, p. 465. The authors suggest that decrease in the amount of revealed abuse was due to a combination of changed attitudes and norms and overt behaviour.

79/ See Australia where comprehensive phone-in surveys have been carried out in South Australia, New South Wales, the Northern Territory, Victoria and the Australian Capital Territory. The results of the surveys indicated that there was a high incidence of violence against wives in Australia. Further, results of a survey by the British Medical Research Council of a random group of 286 women to be published in late 1987 reveals that one in four women in Britain have been abused by their husband or lover. Andrews and Brown, op. cit.

80/ C. Benard and E. Schlaffer, "Forms of crisis intervention and types of immediate and structural measures to render assistance to women assaulted in the family", case study on Austria reporting on a three-year study of domestic violence by the Ludwig Boltzmann Institute of Politics, Vienna, prepared for the Expert Group Meeting on Violence in the Family with Special Emphasis on its Effects on Women, Vienna, 8-12 December 1986.

81/ See note 53.

82/ Al-Awadi, op. cit.

83/ Wamalwa, op. cit., Skrobanek, op. cit. A small-scale random survey of 150 women was carried out in Thailand between October and November 1985.

84/ Akande, op. cit.

85/ The author of the Ugandan case study carried out her own survey on the questionnaire model and again domestic violence was found to be a prevalent problem.

86/ Stark, Flitcraft and Frazier, "Medicine and patriarchal violence ...", pp. 461-493.

87/ Gayford, loc. cit., pp. 21-22. See also, V. Binney, G. Harkell and J. Nixon, Leaving Violent Men: A Study of Refuges and Housing for Battered Women (Leeds, Women's Aid Federation, 1981). This team, which studies refuge users in England and Wales, found that 73% of the women had put up with violence for three or more years. 30% had suffered life-threatening attacks or been hospitalized for serious injury such as broken bones, while the rest had been kicked, pushed into fires, thrown against walls, down stairs, punched and had their hair pulled. Similar results were found by Dobash and Dobash in their interviews of women in Scottish refuges.

88/ Al-Awadi, op. cit. Responses to questionnaire.

89/ Wamalwa, op. cit. Newspaper survey.

90/ ISIS Internacional, case study from Chile. Hospital survey.

91/ Freeman, loc. cit., p. 124; Frieze, loc. cit., p. 532.

92/ D. Finkelhor and K. Yllo, "Rape in marriage: a sociological view", a paper presented at Rape: A Drama From Two Perspectives, Tynnigo, Sweden, 3-7 June, E. Hedlund, ed. (Stockholm, I.P.P.F., 1985), p. 57.

93/ L. Walker, The Battered Woman (New York, Harper and Row, 1977), pp. 51-54.

94/ The Police Foundation, Domestic Violence and the Police: Studies in Detroit and Kansas City (National Institute of Justice: 1977).

95/ New South Wales Bureau of Crime Statistics and Research, "New South Wales homicides cleared up by the police between 1968 and 1981", in Domestic Violence, Australian Law Reform Commission Report No. 30 (Canberra, A.G.P.S., 1986), pp. 1-2. Similar statistics are available from the United States where the Uniform Crime Reports indicate that one third of female homicide victims are killed by husbands or boyfriends. <u>Uniform Crime Reports for 1983</u> (Washington, D.C., Government Printing Office, 1984).

96/ MacLeod, <u>Wife Battering in Canada ...</u>, pp. 10-11.

97/ Shamim, <u>op. cit.</u>

98/ Wamalwa, <u>op. cit.</u> Survey of newspaper reports.

99/ Skrobanek, <u>op. cit.</u> Survey of newspaper reports.

100/ P. Jaffe and others, "Emotional and physical health problems of battered women", <u>Canadian Journal of Psychiatry</u>, No. 31, 1986, p. 625.

101/ Walker, <u>op. cit.</u>; E. Hilberman and F. Munson, "Sixty battered women", <u>Victimology</u>, No 2, 1978, pp. 460, 464-465.

102/ Hilberman and Munson, <u>loc. cit.</u>

103/ Hilberman and Munson, <u>loc. cit.</u> See also Colombian case study, which indicates that such women often have a severe lack of self-esteem (Plata, <u>op. cit.</u>).

104/ United States Attorney-General's Task Force on Family Violence, Final Report, p. 101. MacLeod, <u>Battered But Not Beaten ...</u>, p. 31: 14% of the women in MacLeod's study sample reported a history of alcohol abuse and 8%, drug abuse.

105/ National Clearing House on Domestic Violence, <u>Wife Abuse in the Medical Setting: An Introduction for Health Personnel</u> (Washington, D.C., 1981), p. 20.

106/ Shamim, <u>op. cit.</u>, p. 4.

107/ H. Singh, case study from India (New Delhi, National Institute of Social Defence, Ministry of Welfare), p. 13.

108/ New South Wales Bureau of Crime Statistics and Research, "New South Wales homicides cleared up ...", pp. 1-2. L. Bacon and R. Lansdowne, "Women who kill husbands - the problem of defence", paper delivered at the 52nd ANZAAS Conference, Sydney, 1982.

109/ Department of Justice, Federal Bureau of Investigation, <u>Crime in the United States, 1980: 1981</u>, Uniform Crime Reports (Washington, D.C., Government Printing Office), pp. 333 and 339.

110/ Skrobanek, <u>op. cit.</u>

111/ E. Stark and A. Flitcraft, "Woman-battering, child abuse and social heredity: what is the relationship?", in <u>Marital Violence</u>, N. Johnson, ed., Sociological Review Monography No. 31 (London, Routledge and Kegan Paul, 1985), pp. 147, 159-160.

112/ <u>Ibid</u>. See also, MacLeod, <u>Battered But Not Beaten ...</u>, pp. 32-33, which indicates that there is a high level of child abuse in families where the woman is abused. In such cases, the abuser is most often the man, although it may sometimes be the woman.

113/ D. A. Wolfe and others, "Children of battered women: the relation of child behaviour to family violence and maternal stress", Journal Consulting and Clinical Psychology, No. 53, 1985, pp. 657-664.

114/ Plata, op. cit., p. 15. The police study also revealed that 32 children of such families were beggars, 122 such children were drugged, there were 389 prostitutes and 127 insane adults all emerging from situations of family violence.

115/ H. M. Hughes and S. J. Barad, "Psychological functioning of children in a battered woman's shelter: a preliminary investigation", American Journal of Orthopsychiatry, No. 53, 1983, p. 525.

116/ E. C. Herrenkohl, R. C. Herrenkohl and L. J. Toedter, "Perspectives on the intergenerational transmission of abuse", in The Dark Side of Families: Current Family Violence Research, D. Finkelhor and others, eds. (Beverly Hills, Sage, 1983).

117/ Stark and Flitcraft, "Women-battering ...", p. 165. See also C. D. Spinellis, Greek case study (Athens, University of Athens, Faculty of Law), p. 7, where it is suggested that victims of violence become victimisers themselves, but it is acknowledged that findings are unsystematically collected.

118/ P. Jaffe and others, "Similarities in behavioral and social maladjustment among child victims and witnesses to family violence", American Journal of Orthopsychiatry, No. 56, 1986, p. 142.

119/ D. G. Fischer, Family Relationship Variables and Programs Influencing Juvenile Delinquency (Ottawa, Canada, 1985), p. 41. See also D. O. Lewis and others, "Homicidally-aggressive young children: neuropsychiatric and experimental correlates", American Journal of Psychiatry, No. 140, 1983, p. 148, which found that a father's violence towards the mother was the most significant contributing factor in 21 homicidally aggressive children.

120/ "Wife beating the silent crisis", Time Magazine, September 1983, p. 23.

121/ Intimate Victims: A Study of Violence Among Friends and Relatives (Washington, D.C., Department of Justice, Bureau of Justice Statistics, 1980).

122/ National Clearinghouse on Domestic Violence, Wife Abuse in the Medical Setting ..., pp. 7-9, found in a survey of 2,676 women using the emergency sur- gical service at an urban hospital, 21% had a history of abuse while it was revealed in a sample of 1,155 women using the simple emergency service, that women at risk of abuse were twice as likely to use the service.

123/ MacLeod, Battered But Not Beaten ..., p. 35. MacLeod further indicates that the 1985 budget for the 106 Canadian women's refuges was $C 18.3 million and extrapolates this figure across all the refuges in Canada, and adds to it the costs of police services and concludes that the direct costs to the Canadian taxpayer for the two most obvious forms of crisis intervention is at least $C 72 million per year.

124/ M.D.A. Freeman, "Legal ideologies, patriarchal precedents and domestic violence", in State, Law and Family (London, Tavistock, 1984), p. 69.

125/ Ibid., p. 52.

126/ Pahl, op. cit., pp. 187-188.

127/ Dobash and Dobash, Violence Against Wives ..., p. 15. See also M.D.A. Freeman, "Violence against women: does the legal system provide solutions or itself constitute the problem?", British Journal of Law and Society, No. 7, 1980, p. 216.

128/ Hilberman and Munson, loc. cit., p. 460.

129/ J. Renvoize, Web of Violence: A Study of Family Violence (London, Routledge and Kegan Paul, 1978).

130/ Gelles, Family Violence ...

131/ J. J. Gayford, "Wife battering: a preliminary survey of 100 cases", British Medical Journal, No. 1, 1975, p. 194.

132/ P. D. Scott, "Battered wives", British Journal of Psychiatry, No. 125, 1974, p. 433.

133/ Pahl, op cit., p. 9.

134/ See, for example, Domestic Violence Phone-In Report (Adelaide, Australia, Women's Information Switchboard, 1980); Report on Phone-In on Domestic Violence (Victoria, Australia, 1985).

135/ Stojanowska, op. cit.

136/ S. Ranck and S. Toft, "Domestic violence in an urban context with rural comparisons", in Domestic Violence in Urban Papua New Guinea, Occasional Paper No. 19 (Boroko, Law Reform Commission of Papua New Guinea, 1986), p. 3.

137/ Simi, op. cit. See also Report in Conference on Alcohol Related Problems on Pacific Island Countries, sponsored by the South Pacific Commission and the World Health Organization, Noumea, New Caledonia, 9-13 September 1985. This Conference stressed the link between alcohol abuse and domestic violence in the Pacific.

138/ Mukasa-Kikonyogo, op. cit.

139/ ISIS Internacional, case study from Chile.

140/ Al-Awadi, op. cit.

141/ Plata, op. cit.

142/ J. Downey and J. Howell, Wife Battering - A Review and Preliminary Enquiry into Local Incidents, Needs and Resources (Vancouver, B.C., Social Policy and Research Department, United Way of Greater Vancouver and the Non-Medical Use of Drugs Directorate, National Department of Health and Welfare), p. 56.

143/ L. H. Bowker, Beating Wife-Beating (Lexington, Massachussetts, 1983), p. 467.

144/ Downey and Howell, op. cit.

145/ Gelles, The Violent Home ...

146/   R. Epstein, R. Ng and J. Trebble, <u>The Social Organisation of Family Violence: An Ethnography of Immigrant Experience in Vancouver</u> (Vancouver, B.C., Women's Research Centre, 1978), p. 27.

147/   Straus, Gelles and Steinmetz, <u>Behind Closed Doors ...</u>.

148/   <u>Ibid</u>., p. 100.

149/   <u>Ibid</u>., p. 113.

150/   W. Stacey and A. Shupe, <u>The Family Secret: Domestic Violence in America</u> (Boston, Beacon Press, 1983), p. 93.

151/   See also Gelles, <u>The Violent Home ...</u>; J. J. Gayford, "Battered wives", <u>Medical Science and Law</u>, No. 15, 1975, p. 237; B. F. Steele, "Violence within the family", in <u>Child Abuse and Neglect: The Family and the Community</u>, R. E. Helfer and C. H. Kempe, eds. (Cambridge, Massachussetts, Ballinger, 1976).

152/   D. Potts and S. Herzerberger, "Child abuse: a cross generational pattern of child rearing?", a paper presented at the Annual Meeting of the Midwest Psychological Association, Chicago, May 1979.

153/   Dobash and Dobash, <u>Violence Against Wives ...</u>, p. 22; Stark and Flitcraft, "Woman battering, child abuse ...", p. 155.

154/   <u>Ibid</u>. See also Brienes and Gordon, <u>loc. cit</u>., p. 561, who further argue that the database is likely to be skewed to poor and multi-problem families.

155/   Stark and Flitcraft, "Women battering, child abuse ...".

156/   Dobash and Dobash, <u>Violence Against Wives ...</u>, p. 155.

157/   <u>Ibid</u>. Stark and Flitcraft, "Women battering, child abuse ...".

158/   W. J. Goode, "Force and violence in the family", <u>Journal of Marriage and the Family</u>, No. 33, 1971, p. 624.

159/   A. Storr, <u>Human Aggression</u> (London, Penguin, 1974), p. 95; J. Jobling, "Battered wives: a survey", <u>Social Service Quarterly</u>, No. 47, 1974, p. 146; J. Gayford, "Ten types of battered women", <u>Welfare Officer</u>, No.   , 1976, p. 25.

160/   E. Pizzey and J. Shapiro, <u>Prone to Violence</u> (London, Hamlyn, 1982).

161/   Pahl, <u>op. cit</u>., p. 5. See also Andrews and Brown, <u>op. cit</u>., which reports that of 72 women found to have been involved in a violent relationship, 32 had cohabited with more than one man, but of these only three had been involved in more than one relationship.

162/   Dobash and Dobash, <u>Violence Against Wives ...</u>, p. 135.

163/   <u>Ibid</u>., pp. 135-137; note also Andrews and Brown, <u>op. cit</u>., which investigated 72 abused women who had been culled from a random survey. Of these women, only two ever physically provoked an attack and, far from being "addicted" to or "prone" to violence, most came from families which were neglectful rather than abusive. The researchers concluded that a woman's neglectful family of origin may make her susceptible to involvement in unsatisfactory relationships.

164/ Pizzey, op. cit.

165/ British Association of Social Workers, Discussion document of B.A.S.W. Working Party on Home Violence, Social Work Today, No. 6, 1975, p. 409. See also Gelles, The Violent Home ..., p. 185; MacLeod, Wife Battering in Canada ..., p. 26.

166/ ISIS Internacional, case study from Chile.

167/ Akande, op. cit.

168/ Wamalwa, op. cit.

169/ El Husseiny Zaalouk, op. cit.

170/ Shamim, op. cit.

171/ Wamalwa, op. cit.; Mukasa-Kikonyogo, op. cit.

172/ Singh, op. cit. and Bangladesh Economist, 22 August 1987.

173/ J. E. O'Brien, "Violence in divorce-prone families", Journal of Marriage and the Family, No. 33, 1971, p. 692.

174/ W. J. Goode, "Force and violence in the family", Journal of Marriage and the Family, No. 33, 1971, p. 624.

175/ M. Pagelow, Battered Women: A New Perspective (Dublin, International Sociological Association, 1977).

176/ Toft, op. cit. This monograph contains eight studies of the incidence, causes and approaches to domestic violence in Papua New Guinea. Sexual jealousy is revealed to be one of the major contexts in which such violence is manifested.

177/ Pahl, op. cit., p. 33.

178/ Dobash and Dobash, Violence Against Wives ..., p. 98; M. Roy, ed., Battered Women: A Psychosociological Study of Domestic Violence (London, Van Nostrand Reinhold, 1977).

179/ E. Evason, Hidden Violence (Belfast, Farset Press, 1982).

180/ M. Homer, A. Leonard and R. Taylor, "The burden of dependency", in Marital Violence, N. Johnson, ed., Sociological Review Monograph 31 (London, Routledge and Kegan Paul, 1985), p. 77.

181/ Pahl, op. cit., p. 42.

182/ Ibid., p. 43.

183/ M. Straus, "Sexual inequality, cultural norms and wife beating", in Women into Wives, J. R. Chapman and M. Gates, eds. (Beverly Hills, Sage, 1976), p. 59. See also MacLeod, Wife Battering in Canada ..., p. 31: "To understand violence in the family, we must look at the way the family is kept isolated, the woman dependent and family violence legitimated through family roles, mandates and restrictions and through other institutions in their normal operation".

184/ D. Martin, Battered Wives (San Francisco, Glide, 1976); J. Hammer, "Violence and the social control of women", in Power and the State, G. Littlejohn, ed. (London, Croom Helm, 1977); M.D.A. Freeman, "Violence against women: does the legal system provide solutions or itself constitute the problem?", British Journal of Law and Society, No. 7, 1980, p. 215; Scutt, op. cit.; S. Jackson and P. Rushton, "Victims and villains: images of women in accounts of family violence", Women's Studies International Forum, No. 5, 1982, p. 7.

185/ Dobash and Dobash, Violence Against Wives ...; Freeman, "Violence against women ...", p. 215.

186/ Singh, op. cit.

187/ Wu Han, case study from China (Shanghai, Criminology and Crime Investigation Department, East China Institute of Law and Politics).

188/ El Husseiny Zaalouk, op. cit.; Akande, op. cit.

189/ Mukasa-Kikonyogo, op. cit.; Al-Awadi, op. cit.; El Husseiny Zaalouk, op. cit.; Plata, op. cit.

190/ Akande, op. cit.

191/ Al-Awadi, op. cit.; Mukasa-Kikonyogo, op. cit.; Wamalwa, op. cit.; Akande, op. cit.; El Husseiny Zaalouk, op. cit.

192/ Pahl, op. cit., pp. 18-19.

193/ M.D.A. Freeman, Violence in the Home (Farnborough, Saxon House, 1979), pp. 141-142.

194/ Dobash and Dobash, "Wives the "appropriate" victims ...", p. 426.

195/ R. Leonard and E. MacLeod, Marital Violence: Social Construction and Social Service Response (University of Warwick, 1980).

196/ C. Benard, "Patterns of violence against women in the family", Working Paper on the Nature and Effects of Physical Violence and Coercion Against Women in the Family, Expert Group Meeting on Violence in the Family with Special Emphasis on its Effects on Women, Vienna, 8-12 December 1986.

197/ Developing societies are typically in a state of transition. This may go some way to explain the prevalence of domestic violence in such societies. See Indian, Chinese, Colombian and Kenyan case studies.

198/ M. Straus, "A sociological perspective in the prevention of wife beating", in Social Causes of Husband-Wife Violence, M. Straus and G. Hotaling, eds. (Minneapolis, University of Minnesota Press, 1980), pp. 211-232.

199/ Brienes and Gordon, loc. cit., p. 503.

200/ Mukasa-Kikonyogo, op. cit.; Wamalwa, op. cit.

Part Two

TYPES OF RESPONSE TO VIOLENCE

It has been indicated, in Part One that in all countries of the world, the abuse of women within the family is widespread, that the consequences of such abuse are serious and that it is not a modern phenomenon. It has only been recently, however, that countries have started to acknowledge the issue as an important one and have attempted to address the plight of women victims of abuse.

Acknowledgement of the issue did not take place simultaneously in different countries. Some countries recognized the problem earlier than others and have had a longer period in which to develop strategies to confront violence against women within the home. However, even in those countries that claim to have recognized the issue earlier rather than later, much work remains to be done as even the earliest serious recognition occurred only within the last 20 years (see page 11).

Responses to violence against women in the family are coloured in all societies by a number of important social values. The first is that the family is a private place, a source of comfort and nurturance for its members and as such should be regarded as sacred. This value is so important that it is enshrined in international human rights instruments 1/ that guarantee the right to a private and family life, a home and correspondence. 2/

While privacy and autonomy in family life are desirable to protect ordinary people against unnecessary intrusions of the State, the concept of family privacy has two important negative effects in the context of family violence. First, members are severely constrained from seeking help outside the family, because to do so would amount to an admission by the individual family that it was not providing the ideal comfort and nurturance which, given the societal pressure to keep family troubles within the home, is a shameful failure. 3/ Secondly, intervention from outsiders, even in the face of clear family dysfunction, is discouraged. Violence within the family, therefore, is ignored or trivialized because acknowledgement of its existence would infringe the privacy of the family.

Closely allied to the value of family privacy is the concept of the family as an institution. This presupposes that the family is an institution built on love and security and, as such, is the ideal environment for the upbringing of children and the individual growth of its members. Again, while this may well be the case, this value leads to efforts to sustain the family unit even where the woman is being treated violently by her partner. The maintenance of the family as a unit may thus take precedence over the safety of the woman.

Finally, a certain level of family violence is condoned by most societies. Physical discipline of children is allowed and indeed, often encouraged, and a large number of countries allow physical moderate chastisement of a wife or, if they do not do so now, have done so within the last 100 years (see page 11). Allied with this condonation is a denial by many that violence against a wife is a serious issue that may have long-lasting effects for the woman, her assailant and her children, and a widespread belief that women provoke violence and, indeed, enjoy, or can tolerate, a certain level of violence from their spouses.

These values, which legitimate a certain level of wife abuse, recur as themes when strategies to confront violence against women within the home are considered. They, further, combine, to a large degree, to undermine strategies that have been introduced. Nevertheless, steps have been taken towards the amelioration of the position of victims of such abuse and the ultimate eradication of the objectionable conduct.

The issue of wife abuse has been seen primarily as a problem that requires legal solutions, thus much of Part Two is devoted to the exploration of legal responses that have been made. Chapter I investigates the policies that law-makers have considered and adopted in dealing with the issue, policies in which the police, who are the subject of chapter II, play a crucial role. Chapter III outlines the formal legal methods that have been used to confront the violence, concluding with an investigation of the role of the court and its attendant actors: prosecutors, magistrates and judges. Finally, it describes the less formal legal approaches, for example, diversion and conciliation and mediation schemes, that have been utilized.

The responses of others who may be involved in the problem are then considered by examining the approach of the health and welfare sectors. It concludes with a survey of community responses to the issue, concentrating on the role of women's groups and the "shelter" movement.

I. THE LAW: DEALING WITH VIOLENCE THROUGH THE LEGAL SYSTEM

Although the legal system has been viewed as the basic tool in the treatment of violence against women in the family, the policies that those involved in law-making and the conduct of the legal system have pursued when grappling with the issue have not been uniform over time or from country to country. Fundamentally, in all countries where wife abuse has emerged as a serious issue, those involved in the law have been forced to confront the central question of whether the penal or criminal justice system is appropriate in the management of domestic violence.

Two divergent views have emerged. The first, and perhaps now dated, view is that in the management of wife abuse, the criminal law is at best a blunt instrument. An approach focusing on mediation or conciliation, or a model that is therapeutic or welfare-oriented, is therefore advocated, and the intervention of law enforcers with arrest, prosecution and sentencing is avoided. The criminal law is confined to the most serious cases of abuse or, in other words, is seen as a "last resort".

The second, and more current, view sees domestic assault, notwithstanding the fact that it takes place within the family and occurs between intimates, as a crime. As such, its advocates demand that wife assault should be treated no differently from any other crime.

These two divergent philosophies underpin all legal responses to domestic violence. In effect, the responses that have been made move along a continuum at one end of which is a purely welfare, or therapeutic approach, and at the other end of which is an approach that advocates criminal sanction in all cases. It is crucial therefore to explore the basis of each philosophy.

Certainly, forceful arguments can be raised and are raised against the use of the criminal law in the domestic context. The criminal law is punitive, rather than rehabilitative. It looks to past conduct and is rarely concerned with future behaviour. 4/ As such, it is rare for criminal justice systems to provide treatment programmes that could, for example, train the man to control his aggression. The criminal law depends for its effectiveness on the actors involved in the penal system - the police, prosecutors and judges - who notoriously have failed to perceive wife abuse as a criminal issue and therefore refuse to arrest, prosecute and convict (see page 68). Even when these actors act in all good faith, a criminal conviction may not follow, perhaps because evidence is difficult to obtain or insufficient to carry the burden of proof. If the violent man is acquitted, even on a technicality, he may continue to victimize his wife. Even if he is convicted and sentenced, this sentence is likely to amount only to a fine or a short period in custody. Any sentence will inevitably penalize his victim. In all probability, a fine will be paid out of joint family finances and imprisonment may cause financial hardship because the breadwinner is incarcerated or may lose his employment. Moreover, even where a husband is sanctioned by imprisonment, this will only temporarily relieve his victim's situation. She may well be confronted with an even more violent man on his release. 5/

Others who argue against the criminal justice approach point to the fact that it has the capacity to harm the family disastrously. This, they suggest, is particularly true in traditional societies where the wife would be isolated by her extended family and the husband's kin would revenge themselves on her. 6/

In short, critics of a criminal justice approach point to the limitations of the criminal law as a means of rehabilitation, the current failure of its personnel to act in accordance with its spirit, its technical limitations and the adverse effect it can have on the victim and her family. Finally, they point to research which reveals a high success rate in reducing domestic abuse by mediation. 7/

Against that, cogent arguments are made to advocate preserving the criminal law in the domestic context and indeed, making it the linchpin upon which to hang the treatment of abuse.

Advocates of the criminal justice model acknowledge that the criminal process as currently practised in the context of abuse may well be defective. This, they argue, is merely a reflection of social values that have historically denied the existence of or trivialized violence against women in the home. They point, first, to the symbolic power of the law. Arrest, prosecution and conviction, with punishment, is a process that carries the clear condemnation of society for the conduct of the abuser and acknowledges his personal responsibility for the activity. It indicates that crime within the home is not merely a social problem, but is as much a crime as crime in the street. It serves, therefore, to place the interests of the victim in a central position, refusing to subordinate her protection to the preservation of the relationship or her family which, they argue, is in contra-distinction to the counselling model that seeks to re-establish the relationship and preserve the family. Further, they believe that the current neutrality of the criminal justice system subtly encourages assailants and unfairly places equal blame on the battered woman for being involved in the violence. In short, they suggest that the criminal approach, unlike the counselling model, refuses to accept or condone any abuse of women in the home and thus does not victimize the individual woman further.

The symbolic and educative role of the law has important implications for the ultimate elimination of violence against women in the home, as the law can serve to shape and change attitudes to the objectionable behaviour. Moreover, the value of the criminal justice system in the management of abuse is, its advocates argue, more real than symbolic. Some research studies reveal that intervention by the criminal justice system is the most effective mechanism for stopping acts of violence in the short term and also in the long term. The criminal justice mode, which draws on the coercive powers of the State, is, they suggest, therefore, the only approach that guarantees immediate safety for a victim of abuse and has the capacity to retrain assailants and thereby reduce recidivism. Here proponents rely on mounting evidence that involvement of the police in their law enforcement role has a substantial impact on the man's behaviour. They point first to research which reveals that arrest with its associated and intimidating procedures at the police station reduces the risk of recidivism in the abuser, and secondly to the positive effects of a policy of mandatory prosecution in the management of abuse.

Clear evidence exists which indicates that if abuse is allowed to continue unchecked it escalates and may ultimately lead to the death of the woman. Thus, one study reveals that police had been called at least once before in 85 per cent of spousal abuse and homicide cases and in half of the cases where homicide ultimately occurred, the police had responded previously five times or more. 8/ Given this finding, the importance of the police role in stemming abuse connot be underrated. Further research suggests that while any action by the police may curtail further abuse, 9/ arrest is most effective as a future deterrent.

Here, the results of the Minneapolis Domestic Violence Experiment, 10/ which was conducted in 1981 under the sponsorship of the United States Institute of Justice and carried out by the Police Foundation in co-operation

with the Minneapolis Police Department, are particularly revealing. The
Experiment was designed specifically to assess which of three police responses
- conducting informal mediation between parties involved in the domestic dispute, ordering the suspect to leave the residence for eight hours, or arresting
the suspect - was the most effective in preventing subsequent assault.

During a six-month period, the research revealed that 19 per cent of
those involved in mediation and 24 per cent of those ordered to leave repeated
the assault, but only 10 per cent of those who were arrested indulged in further violence towards their spouses. 10/ These results led the researchers to
conclude that "an arrest should be made unless there are good, clear reasons
why an arrest would be counter-productive". 11/ The researchers did, however,
enter a number of caveats suggesting that the implication that arrest was the
best method of management of wife abuse was not inevitable. Thus, they noted
that their sample size was small, amounting to 314 victims, and may well have
excluded some types of person for whom arrest would be totally counter-
productive. They pointed to the fact that the Minneapolis justice system was
unusual because arrest incorporated overnight incarceration, which itself may
have had a greater effect on recidivism. Further, they indicated that their
experiment also included intensive interviews with victims during a six-month
period, which may have had a surveillance effect on abusers. Finally, they
warned that different effects of police action in domestic violence cases may
follow in different cultural contexts.

The Minneapolis experiment was replicated by Berk and Newton in 1985 12/
when results consistent with the original research were produced. Notwithstanding the specific caveats of the original researchers, mandatory arrest in
domestic violence cases has been introduced in a number of jurisdictions 13/
and is advocated by many concerned in the field of domestic violence.

Similar positive effects in the management of abuse are believed to follow where the police are not simply instructed to arrest but, rather, are
mandated to lay criminal charges against the abusive man. Here the research
of Jaffe, Wolfe, Telford and Austin 14/ into the impact of a policy directing
an urban police force in Canada to lay criminal charges in cases of wife
assault where reasonable and probable grounds existed that the assault took
place, rather than abdicating this responsibility to the wife, as is more
common, is critical. 15/

The research into the charging policy, which was introduced in London,
Ontario, in 1981, was measured against data available from 1979, 18 months
before the formal policy was introduced. The study addressed the response and
attitude of police officers, the perception of victims of wife assault and the
recurrence of the violence as reported by the victim and the formal police and
court record. It revealed that there had been a dramatic increase in the
police laying assault charges in response to the directive: indeed, there had
been a radical shift to the police rather than the victim laying charges and
the proportion of cases heard in the criminal court rose from 1 in 16 to 3 out
of 4 cases. Although the police officers were of the view that the new policy
had had little effect in reducing family violence, the perception of the victims of abuse was otherwise, and this perception was confirmed by evidence
available from the formal police and court records. Hence, a vast majority of
the victims indicated that the police and court process played a significant
role in reducing or terminating the violence irrespective of whether their
spouse was held guilty of an offence. This was supported by the actual level
of physical abuse reported after the police intervention as well as the number
of police attendances and court proceedings related to the violence. In sum,
the research revealed that victims were at greater risk of renewed threats or
assault if charges were not laid.

In recent years, the number of jurisdictions that have been convinced by advocacy for the criminal justice model in the management of abuse has grown. These jurisdictions have firmly indicated that domestic violence is a crime and have followed this commitment with specific legal provisions, such as mandatory arrest and prosecution, that guarantee it. Thus, since 1983 Canadian police have been directed to lay criminal charges in all cases of domestic assault, even where the victim would prefer to withdraw the complaint, 16/ a policy that has also been introduced in a number of states in America and in New South Wales, Australia. 17/ Prosecutors and Crown attorneys have been ordered to pursue such prosecutions and to exercise caution when asked by the victim to withdraw charges that have been laid either by the police or the victim herself.

Despite the current popularity of the criminal model in the management of domestic violence, it is critical that any policy that is pursued and any philosophy that underpins it should take into account the cultural, economic and political realities of the situation. Certainly, in most systems, physical, sexual and some varieties of emotional abuse of a woman within the family are crimes. However, it is impossible to ignore the fact that these crimes take place within the family between persons who are emotionally and financially involved with one another. Any approach to domestic assault that fails to acknowledge the singular nature of the crime and that is not accompanied by an attempt to provide support for the victim, and indeed, help for the abuser, will be doomed to failure. Thus, any policy of arrest in a vacuum unaccompanied by complementary changes in other legal procedures both pre- and post-arrest will be ineffective. Vigorous arrest policies without energetic charging and conviction policies can only provoke anger and lead to further violence and, moreover, may engender cynicism and disillusion in the police. So, also, charging policies and conviction policies that fail to take account of the particular context of the jurisdiction may be provocative and ultimately ineffective. Thus, it is important to learn from the experience of London, Ontario, which introduced the first charging policy, but in a context that provided support. There, the police force funds a family consultant service that provides a 24 hour crisis intervention service and also provides police training in how to deal with wife battering. Moreover, a community context exists that includes a battered women's advocacy clinic providing legal and emotional counselling for women, as well as a treatment group for men who batter.

Any policy to manage wife abuse must thus be appropriate to the particular context into which it is being introduced. Reformers should note, for example, that traditional societies and communities may find strategies based on mediation and conciliation more familiar and more appropriate to their context than strategies based on the criminal model. Further, no matter what strategy is introduced, it is essential that it should be flexible and not rigidly applied. This is particularly true in multi-cultural societies where cultural differences may mean that certain groups of women are confronted with particular difficulties. For example, it must be appreciated that aboriginal women may be distrustful of the dominant culture's justice system in general, and criminal justice system in particular, 18/ an attitude that may be shared by immigrant women. This distrust may mean that such women are reluctant to co-operate in any strategy. Moreover, no matter what model is adopted it must be introduced with sensitivity and explanation. Here, an important lesson can be learned from the experience of Canada, where rigid application of the criminal justice model has resulted in the imprisonment of some battered women for contempt of court because they have failed to testify against their spouses. 19/

It is clear, therefore, that no matter what approach is adopted to the issue of wife abuse it must be appropriate to the cultural context, it cannot be introduced in isolation, and it must accommodate the fact that wife abuse is not like any other crime. It must further be appreciated that no one woman is like another and that all women have different needs, and thus any approach must be flexible.

In the final analysis, perhaps the ideal approach to the management of wife abuse is best summarized by the Australian Law Reform Commission:

"It is not impossible to accommodate both the criminal and the counselling approach. When it is said that domestic violence offenders must be treated in exactly the same way as other offenders it does not necessarily mean that they should inevitably be gaoled. Other offenders are treated by the criminal justice system in a flexible way which takes into account many factors in deciding how the criminal process should proceed and what punishment is appropriate to the particular case." [20]

II. THE POLICE ROLE

In many ways, the important key to a country's response to violence against women is the police response. The police is the only agency that offers the woman a combination of the coercive power of the State and accessibility. In most countries, the only service available to battered women 24 hours a day and seven days a week, apart from hospital accident units, is the police. Moreover, unlike other social services, the police force offers an emergency telephone system and comprehensive geographical coverage. As such, particularly in view of the fact that many incidents of wife abuse occur in the evening or at weekends, when families are together and alcohol is more likely to be consumed, 21/ the police can be expected to be the first and major contact for many women. 22/

Although the police role is critical, the literature that exists, stemming, again, mainly from Britain and North America, indicates that, in general, police response to the issue has been viewed as inadequate. Thus, it is alleged that both the immediate and subsequent reaction of police to an incident of domestic assault is inappropriate and uninformed.

The criticism of police response centres on the following. Police are not seen to offer the woman adequate protection from the violent man, underestimating the violence and fear of violence and dismissing some appeals for help because they are of the view that there are insufficient grounds for intervention. They are reluctant to intervene in domestic disturbances because they place greater value on privacy and on marriage rights than on the woman's right to freedom of assault and fear of assault. Frequently, they subscribe to the view that the woman probably provoked the violence in some way. They are loath to act and lack interest in a case if they do not see it leading to a successful prosecution and, finally, they are unaware of sources of help and support that could be available to the woman. Thus, for example, Binney and her colleagues 23/ who interviewed 59 women in England who had left their violent husbands found that in 8 per cent of the cases, 25 of which involved life threatening attacks, the police, when called, did not come to the scene of the violence at all, in 51 per cent the police said it was a domestic dispute and no practical help was given, in 17 per cent the man was charged with assault or breaching an injunction, while in 20 per cent, practical help was given in that the man was taken away for the night or the woman was referred to a refuge. 24/

Studies indicate that the police practice in cases of domestic violence is to attempt to mediate or counsel the parties and achieve reconciliation rather than to fulfil a role of law enforcement. Police, therefore, have traditionally preferred not to arrest the violent spouse, where in other cases arrest would be automatic, even when the woman requests such arrest 25/ except where the violence is very severe 26/ or there is some other important variable, for example, where the man is drunk, 27/ belligerent towards the police, 28/ or where the neighbours have complained. 29/ Pursuance of the mediating, rather than law enforcement, role is particularly likely in situations where the parties are married and living together. Attempts at mediation will also occur in other domestic circumstances, but if the parties are cohabitees or if they are living apart police are more willing to use their law enforcement powers. 30/

Certainly, mediation is the preferred response in developing countries, for example, in Egypt, women who are the victims of abuse are referred to the social worker at the police station, 31/ in Malaysia, 32/ Nigeria, 33/ and Thailand 34/ the police attempt to conciliate and dissuade the woman from taking the matter to court, an approach that is also taken in Greece. 35/

The traditional police response stressing peace-keeping, rather than law enforcement, often stems from recruit training which in many cases indicates that violence in domestic circumstances is less a criminal than a social issue. 36/ Training perspectives are then crystallized by other factors. Experience of police officers in cases of domestic violence is frequently frustrating. For example, despite routine beatings, victims remain in violent relationships and even refuse to assist in the prosecution of their abusers. Officers, therefore, explain their failure to act in a law enforcement mode as the result of the reluctance of victims to press charges in the initial phases of the investigation and their later reluctance to give evidence in court. 37/ Police, who are generally not attuned to the dynamics of abusive relationships and thus not alert to issues of dependency, fear, responsibility for the children of the union and general helplessness, may conclude that victims are attention-grabbing masochists. 37/ Again, some police, like many others, see family violence, which provides them with some of their most dangerous (see page 22) and least liked work, as a part of family life, 38/ which they believe should not be part of police work at all. 39/ In some situations, furthermore, the police may merely reflect the societal view that a man has the right to beat his wife. 40/

There is no doubt that the police role in wife assault is ambiguous and the task very difficult. Much of the ambiguity arising from the conflicting view of their role as counsellor or law enforcer is a reflection of ambiguities in society itself. Part of society regards wife abuse as criminal activity, while part is of the view that a man has a right to do as he wishes with his wife. Again, part of society thinks whatever happens within the confines of the home should be private and not open to public scrutiny, while the other part is of the view that a crime is a crime no matter where it occurs. This ambiguity operates again when the responses of other actors in the legal structures - prosecutors, crown attorneys, magistrates and judges - are considered. 41/ In the final analysis, the ambiguity of the police role is a reflection of societal attitudes that are prepared to trivialize the abuse of women in the home, removing it from the purview of the criminal system and relegating it to the ragbag of social problems.

While the ambiguity that colours police response will ultimately only be resolved with total societal condemnation of wife abuse, much of the difficulty that confronts the police in the management of the area results from problems that are remediable in the short term.

First, much police ineffectiveness results from inadequate or unclear legal powers, such as police power of entry, police power to arrest and police power to release on bail. Secondly, clearly defined policies towards the issue have not been developed, thereby leaving the individual operational officer with an open discretion to act in individual cases that is uninformed and unclear. Finally, little training or priority is given to recruits and officers to prepare them for cases of family violence, even though these cases constitute a large proportion of an officer's work and often prove dangerous. Any untrained individual operating in an area that is regarded as low priority, and thus unimportant, will have difficulty appreciating the needs of the victim, the characteristics of the battered and the importance of accurate police response.

Four areas of the police role, therefore, are considered below. These areas are as follows: police powers of entry onto private premises in cases of domestic violence, police power to arrest the suspected offender, the release of the suspected offender on bail, and police training in the area of domestic violence.

A. Police powers of entry

In most countries of the world, the power of the police or others in authority to enter the private premises of an individual is limited. This limitation, which is in accordance with internationally accepted standards of civil liberties, is extremely important as it protects ordinary women and men from arbitrary interference by the State in their private lives. 42/ In the context of domestic abuse, however, the limitation has a capacity to bring about grave harm as it protects the abuser from the scrutiny of those outside the home and sacrifices his victim to the concepts of privacy and autonomy.

While it is important to advocate free entry of law enforcement officials onto private property, and at the same time respect concepts of civil liberties, it is possible to clarify and make more effective police powers of entry in cases of actual and suspected wife assault.

In many systems, police powers of entry onto private premises are limited to cases where they have reasonable grounds to suspect that a breach of peace is occurring or about to occur or to situations where they have been issued with a warrant. In essence, a breach of the peace or a potential breach of the peace cannot be anticipated in circumstances where there is no indication that assault has or is about to occur. Typically, police will be called to a violent scene and will be met by a member of the household who will tell them that no disturbance is occurring or has occurred. The police, unless invited into the household or able to discern breach of the peace, by noise for example, will have no right to enter in the absence of a warrant. 43/ If they do effect entry by trick or by force, they may face consequences such as a legal suit from the occupier or a disciplinary hearing within the force.

Some jurisdictions, disturbed at the danger of too great an emphasis on restrictions of police power in the context of domestic assault, have devised special strategies to meet the problem. Thus, New South Wales, one of the Australian jurisdictions, allows the police to enter premises where they believe on reasonable grounds that a domestic violence offence has recently been or is being committed or is imminent or is likely to be committed in the house if they are invited to do so by any person who apparently lives in the house and they are not forbidden to do so expressly by the occupier. 44/ In simple terms, this provision means that if, for example, a child who appeared to live on the premises asked the police officer into the home and the child's father, the occupier, did not expressly forbid entry, the officer would not need to hear or see evidence of breach of the peace and would not require a warrant for her entry to be legal. A further provision allows the officer to enter the premises even though the occupier refuses such entry, where the officer is invited by the person she believes is or is about to be the victim of violence. 45/ Finally, if the officer is not invited into the home by a resident or the victim, the officer need not waste valuable time in securing a warrant to allow entry, but may assure the short term safety of the victim by acquiring a warrant over the police radio telephone. 46/

While it is true that the radio telephone warrant has rarely been sought in the particular jurisdiction, 47/ it is a device that has important potential in the context of domestic violence. The police power is clarified speedily and thus immediate intervention is possible. At the same time, the potential the device provides for serious violation of civil liberties must not be overlooked. It is critical that such innovative ideas be accompanied by safeguards so that no abuses occur. It is easy to imagine, for example, a police force using such a device to facilitate an illegal search. 48/

B. Powers of arrest

In many ways, the question of the arrest of the offender becomes the
central one in the context of domestic violence. Arrest not only provides
immediate protection for the victim, by virtue of the physical removal of the
offender, but also decides the important issue of policy, that is whether the
law enforcement or counselling/social welfare model is being applied to the
case. This latter point is so because, generally, but not universally (see
pages 71-72) the decision to arrest indicates that the offender will be
charged with a criminal offence and automatically enter the criminal justice
system.

With respect to the issue of arrest, three areas of investigation emerge.
First, whether the law enforcement model is the appropriate response to spouse
abuse; secondly, whether the police have the legal power to arrest; and finally,
if they do have such power, what criteria will govern their decision to arrest
or to choose not to do so.

The question of whether the law enforcement model is appropriate to
domestic violence has already been canvassed (see page 51). This section will
therefore consider the power to arrest and the criteria for arrest.

In many countries, as with police powers of entry, and again as an
essential protection for individual civil liberties, the power of the police
to arrest is strictly controlled, being confined, usually, to situations of
some urgency. In the normal situation, therefore, in most countries, unless
an offender has committed or is in the process of committing a breach of the
peace or a specified crime, a police officer must have a warrant to arrest. 49/
In many jurisdictions, moreover, arrest is discouraged, proceedings by summons
being favoured. 50/ The reasons behind this policy are reasons of civil
liberties and are well stated as follows:

> "Arrest is the deprivation of freedom. The ultimate instrument
> of arrest is force. The customary companions of arrest are ignominy
> and fear. A police practice of arbitrary arrest is a hallmark of
> tyranny. It is plainly of critical importance to the existence and
> protection of personal liberty under the law that the circumstances
> in which a police officer may, without judicial warrant, arrest or
> detain an individual should be strictly controlled, plainly stated
> and readily ascertainable." 51/

The question of whether an officer has power to arrest in a given jurisdiction is a technical one. 52/ Suffice it to say, that in a situation of
domestic violence, police officers are often uncertain whether they have the
legal power to arrest the offender. This may be so even in cases of very
serious violence, perhaps even where the victim is so injured that she
requires hospitalization. 53/

The uncertainty that police may have with respect to their legal power to
arrest in the context of domestic violence is clearly counter-productive. It
is essential that police should be well aware of their rights to remove an
assailant and protect the victim in this very dangerous area of human conflict. 53/
Clarity is crucial, but the further question is whether police should be given
special powers of arrest in this context.

Many researchers advocate that the police should be given very wide
powers of arrest in situations of domestic conflict and that they should be
mandated to implement them. They argue that arrest is the best remedy for

violence against women in the home. It not only provides the woman with
immediate safety, but gives her a feeling of power and gives the man an immediate message that his behaviour is unacceptable, a message that has been
shown to have long-term effects on his future behaviour (see page 52).
Further, arrest gives the woman a period of time when her spouse is absent
that will allow her to sort out her options and plan her future. While these
reasons are cogent, and the interests of the victim of abuse should be the
first priority, it is critical that arrest, which is the ultimate infringement
on the liberty of the individual, is not misused.

Essentially, the central question is that of the purpose of and justification of arrest. The most radical advocates for mandatory arrest in domestic
violence cases offer arrest as a means of deterrence, a "short, sharp shock"
to stop the man's behaviour. 54/ Their opponents argue, however, that to use
arrest in this fashion not only infringes on international human rights standards, some of which are part of the law of many countries, 55/ but also
serves to punish the batterer before his guilt is proven. 56/

These considerations have, it seems, influenced many jurisdictions
because it remains unusual for arrest to be mandatory in domestic violence
cases. 57/ However, police powers to arrest in the situation of wife assault
have been clarified in many countries so that officers are no longer confused
as to their powers. Moreover, in a large number of jurisdictions, civil sanctions in the form of interdicts and injunctions have been introduced and it
has been common to attach a police power of arrest in the event of their
breach (see page 69).

Even in jurisdictions where powers to arrest have been clarified, it is
not uncommon for the police to prefer to mediate rather than arrest. Traditionally, police have avoided arresting in cases of domestic violence, being
of the opinion that the matters were really social work matters and thus
required a softer approach than normal criminal activity. Decisions to arrest
were based on the seriousness of the offence, the wishes of the victim and
other issues, such as the likelihood of conviction and the number of times the
police had been involved before in disturbances between the couple. 58/ These
attitudes remain to colour police response even in situations where arrest
powers have been widened and clarified. Thus, for example, in the United
Kingdom where arrest powers are frequently attached to civil injunctions,
police none the less prefer not to arrest, notwithstanding the fact that they
have clear power to do so, and attempt to take a mediating path. 59/ Often
this is justified on the ground that the woman, even if she has called them
and insists that she would like her attacker prosecuted, will more than likely
withdraw her complaint and the prosecution will thus inevitably fail. Research
that exists suggests that this police perception is inaccurate, there being
no greater rate of withdrawal in cases of domestic violence than in other
cases. 60/

Police arrest patterns in cases of domestic violence are, at base level,
a reflection of force policy, which in turn is a reflection of wider societal
attitudes. If the wider community is committed to a criminal perception of
the conduct and this perception is reflected in prosecution policies and judicial sentencing patterns, the police will be more inclined to exercise their
powers of arrest (see page 52) and training will demand such a response.
Police patterns of arrest can also be affected by social pressure and campaigns and particular vigilance in situations where arrest powers are not
used. Here, several legal actions from the United States, where class actions
have been brought against police commissioners, are particularly to the point.

In <u>Bruno</u> v. <u>Codd</u> 61/ 12 New York City women who had been beaten by their husbands sued the Police Commissioner and others for failing to provide them with protection against their abusive husbands. Specifically, they objected to the implementation of the New York Family Court Act 1962, which had empowered the Family Court to issue injunctions to battered women whose husbands had been violent against them. The maximum penalty, rarely imposed, for violation of the orders, was six months imprisonment. Police routinely refused to arrest the husband unless the wife secured a Family Court order; however, the Family Court refused to issue such orders. The Manhattan Supreme Court refused to dismiss the suit against the Police Commissioner, thus, ultimately, the Police Department entered into a voluntary arrangement with the women to treat wife abuse in the same manner as any other assault, and to remain at the scene of the attack long enough to stop the violence and to secure any necessary medical treatment for the woman.

A similar action was taken in the case of <u>Scott</u> v. <u>Hart</u> 62/ where four women sued on behalf of a class of married and unmarried women in Oakland, California, who, when they telephoned the Oakland Police Department for assistance and protection against physical abuse from the men with whom they were involved, received either no response or one that was inadequate. This, the women argued, was discriminatory on the basis of sex, encouraged violence against women and was based on "biased and archaic" sexist assumptions that what a man does in his home is not the State's business and that a man had a legal right to punish his wife. Again, the Police Department entered into a settlement with the women which entailed a commitment to treat domestic violence like any other criminal behaviour and limited the police discretion to arrest. 63/

C. Bail

In most legal systems, a person who has been arrested on suspicion of an offence can have the right to be released on bail either by the police or by a judicial officer. Frequently, the suspect will be required to lodge a sum of money or produce a person to act as surety, in other words, undertake to forfeit a sum of money if the suspect does not appear.

In many cases of domestic violence, immediate release of the offender may be dangerous for the victim. Therefore, so that the safety of the victim is assured, those who have the power to grant bail must carefully assess the dangerousness of the abuser's conduct and the likelihood of the continuance of the violence. Release of the offender without prior warning to his victim must be avoided at all costs.

While the offender's right to bail is an important part of his civil liberties, his right to release must be weighed up carefully against the right of his victim to be safe. Certain jurisdictions attempts to strike a balance between these two rights by allowing conditions to be attached to bail. Thus, for example, New South Wales allows the police to prohibit the offender from drinking alcohol or from approaching his victim while on bail. 64/ Any breach of the condition gives the police an immediate right to arrest the offender. Still others allow the detention of the offender for a brief period of time, a period sometimes called a cooling-off period. 65/

Attachment of appropriate conditions to bail provides the victim with a modicum of security. They must, however, be amplified by warnings to the offender from the individual granting bail which point out that the offender is alone accountable for his actions and make clear to him that his victim has the full support and protection from the criminal justice system.

D. Training

Although domestic disputes make up a large proportion of police work (see page 56) and although the work is unpleasant, difficult, sometimes dangerous and always stressful 66/ for police officers, and although legal measures ranging from initial arrest to enforcement of orders that may be handed down depend to a large extent on the police, 67/ very few countries provide specific training for police in the area of wife assault or, if they do so, this training is inadequate. 68/

While certainly the effectiveness of intervention by the police will depend to a large extent on the maturity and personality of the officer, training at all levels can help to change police attitudes to domestic assault and can also alert officers to techniques that are appropriate to the issue.

Instilling attitudes so that the police see domestic abuse as a serious issue and not a normal part of family life or a private problem that will not profit from police intervention is a major educational task, that cannot be achieved immediately. Specialized training in the appropriate methods of response to particular battering calls is also crucial. Here the potential officers have to refer the victim to helping agencies, such as medical and legal services and women's refuges should not be underrated (see page 56).

Some countries have introduced police units that have been specially and intensively trained for the purpose of dealing with spousal assault. These units, which are sometimes multi-disciplinary, including social workers, indicate the commitment of a particular community to the plight of an abused woman, but the introduction of such a unit is not possible in all countries and may, indeed, not be appropriate in certain situations. The major difficulty presented by such a unit is that its establishment may be too expensive for small communities and unavailable in all cases in large communities. Care must also be taken in those countries where special domestic violence units are established that training in wife assault cases is still given to all police officers, as in most countries officers are sent to calls on a random basis and not in accordance with special knowledge. Further, it is common for training in issues directly related to women to be confined to female officers. 69/ This, again, must be guarded against as there is no guarantee that the particular officer will be available when an incident occurs.

Allied with the question of training for police officers are the issues of appropriate record keeping and techniques for collecting evidence. Much research indicates that police officers, probably as a reflection of their attitudes to wife assault, either fail to record the fact that they have attended a scene of domestic violence, or if they do so, the record is inadequate. 70/ While attitude change is a long-term goal, the short-term goal of adequate record keeping can be best achieved by devising forms to record wife assault, which officers could be mandated to use by legislation. 71/ Similarly, good techniques for evidence collection can be instilled by the use of prepared kits. 72/

E. Conclusion

For the police the singular nature of the crime of assault on a spouse sets it apart from other categories of criminal activity. The police response to such assaults is a reflection of deeply entrenched social attitudes that tend to trivialize such assaults or at the very most see them as "disturbances" requiring a social work approach.

While it is clear that domestic assault is very different from most other crimes - the victim is usually dependent emotionally, financially and psycho- logically upon her attacker and very often will continue to live or at least maintain contact with him - it is important that the police recognize that their "social work role" should not interfere with their law enforcement role. To apply only unofficial sanctions or none at all is dangerous to the woman and a source of disillusionment to her, leading her to believe that there is no real alternative for her except her current abusive situation. Further, a low-key police approach demonstrates to the husband that his behaviour is not really "illegal" and therefore not truly unacceptable.

Police practice is an important indication of social attitude. If there is serious commitment to the condemnation of domestic violence, it is essen- tial that police practice reflects this commitment. The police must, however, be provided with clear policies and should be assured that the rest of the criminal justice system is co-ordinated to support these policies. Their legal rights in the context of the crime must be clarified and they must be assured of prosecutorial and judicial support.

Studies indicate that clear policy guidelines issued to police and backed up by appropriate supports encourage police to act decisively in the context of domestic violence. Thus, for example, in London, Ontario, it has been found that police are willing to treat wife assaults in the same way they would treat assaults by strangers when force policy dictates such a course and when they are assured, from the community context, that this approach is desirable (see page 53).

The issue of police policy guidelines of this nature creates attitudinal change in officers, as does education and training. This change will, how- ever, be slow. In some countries it has been concluded that change by policy guidelines and education may be far too slow and more radical solutions are required. Perhaps the most appealing and innovative strategy has been devised in Brazil.

In Brazil, a Women's Police Station opened in São Paulo on 7 August 1985 with the specific task of dealing with the problems of violence against women. The station, totally staffed by women - clerks, typists, operational and desk officers - was dedicated to treating female complainants of all forms of vio- lence with dignity, it being believed that Brazilian male police officers usually treated female complainants with disrespect. The station proved to be very popular and was seen as the most effective contribution to the campaign against violence against women in Brazil, providing immediate and long-term help for victims in the form of protection and advice. Indeed, at the present time there are 27 such stations throughout Brazil and any victim who goes to another station can request to be referred to a Woman's Police Station. 73/

In other countries special bureaucratic systems have been established to monitor police response. Thus, in New South Wales, 74/ a Domestic Violence Programme Officer position has been introduced into the Office of the Police Commissioner with the specific mandate of monitoring the response of 74 divi- sions in the jurisdiction. Finally, experimentation with various approaches of policing domestic violence has occurred in Canada.

In London, Ontario, therefore, all police receive general training in crisis intervention and all have access to a family consultant service that is available in cases of domestic violence to act with the police. Similarly in Regina, Kingston and Vancouver a police/social worker team attend incidents of family violence.

No matter what strategy is introduced to ameliorate police response to domestic violence, however, such response will not change in isolation. All agents in related parts of the criminal justice system and the social services/mental health systems must provide adequate back-up for the police. In short, the response must be co-ordinated and multi-faceted to be effective.

III. LEGAL RESPONSES

In most jurisdictions a woman who is the victim of violence in the home has at her disposal a number of legal remedies. They are, in short, matrimonial relief, a suit for a civil wrong and recourse to the criminal law. In a number of countries, these remedies have been augmented with innovative reforms aimed specifically at wife abuse.

It is extremely important for a victim of such abuse to have access to legal solutions. However, the effect of the law must not be overestimated and, certainly, law reform must not be used as a smokescreen to hide the need for fundamental changes in society.

Domestic violence is not simply a legal problem. It is also a social problem that the legal system cannot eliminate by itself. Attitudes towards the role of women must also change. Further, legal remedies may prove to be blunt instruments when dealing with certain types of abusive conduct. Thus, while legal solutions such as divorce or injunctions or interdicts or recourse to the criminal law may be appropriate to stop physical violence or harassment, the law is not equipped to deal with obsessive jealousy or cautious tormenting.

Legal remedies may also prove to be inadequate. There are complex reasons for this. First, the ideology of the law insists that there is an appropriate balance struck between the needs of the victim and the rights of others in the community, including offenders. There is, thus, a continuing tension between civil liberties and the victim's protection and an ambivalence towards the appropriateness of legal and police intervention into the family. Secondly, legal remedies are frequently undermined by the gap that exists between formal legal rights and the law in practice.

Enforcement of the law depends to a large degree on the exercise of police discretion, while interpretation of the law is left to judges and magistrates. 97/ As such, the utilization and effectiveness of legal remedies depend on the commitment of the police, prosecutors and the judiciary to the spirit of the law (see pages 56 and 71-72).

Although the limitations of legal procedures in the task of relieving the needs of battered women must be recognized, legal intervention in the cycle of domestic violence is vitally important. Legal provisions can go some way towards ensuring the short-term safety of the battered woman and, just as importantly, play a symbolic and educative role.

Legal provisions that provide protection and sanctions against violence in the home reflect society's condemnation of abusive conduct. Such provisions indicate that the behaviour is intolerable and that perpetrators will face serious consequences.

The following describes the various legal approaches countries have taken towards the problem of violence against women in the home. Approaches vary from country to country, but fundamentally three legal solutions are available: matrimonial relief (judicial separation and divorce); the criminal law (criminal prosecutions brought by the State or privately and quasi-criminal remedies); and the civil law (actions for a civil wrong and interdicts or injunctions).

A. Matrimonial relief

Ending a marriage by judicial separation or divorce is a remedy for domestic violence in circumstances where the parties are married.

The law relating to matrimonial causes differs from country to country and it is thus impossible to give a short description of the grounds for divorce or judicial separation. In general terms, however, three varieties of marriage law exist. The first is the general law, based on a European model, such as the English common law, Roman law or Roman Dutch common law. The second is customary law. The third is religious law, such as that derived from Muslim law or Canon law. A short description of marriage laws is complicated further by the fact that in some countries parallel systems of legal regulation exist. For example, in Malaysia, those who profess Islam are governed by Muslim law, while those who do not are governed by general law principles, 75/ while in some African countries plural matrimonial causes law exists, so that some are governed by customary principles, others by principles derived from religious law and others by general law principles. 76/

Notwithstanding the fact that there is little uniformity and legal pluralism in matrimonial causes law throughout the jurisdictions of the world, it is possible to make some general remarks about the availability of matrimonial relief in situations where there is violence against women in the home. Thus, it is possible to generalize and assert that in systems where the couple's marriage is governed by customary law, marriages can be dissolved, but such dissolution is discouraged and is a matter between the families of the couple who will first attempt to reconcile them. This is particularly so in customary systems where dissolution of marriage will entail repayment of bride price which has been made by the husband to the father of the bride. 77/ However, although dissolution will be discouraged, persistent physical cruelty on the part of the husband will be accepted as grounds for the dissolution of a customary marriage. 78/ Customary divorce may not, however, be allowed for minor cruelty or emotional abuse.

In some jurisdictions where matrimonial causes law is derived from religious principles, the woman may find divorce to be unavailable. Thus in countries whose law is based on Roman Catholic Canon law, divorce is forbidden and the woman must be content with judicial separation. In jurisdictions where personal law is derived from Islam, a woman may find her right to divorce severly curtailed, but in most she will be able to divorce her husband if he is cruel. 79/

General law principles governing divorce appear to fall into one of three models. The first allows for divorce where the other party is guilty of some form of fault, the second allows for divorce where the marriage has broken down irretrievably and there is some evidence to show this breakdown, evidence that usually is very reminiscent of fault, and, finally, divorce where the marriage has irretrievably broken down either because the parties assert that it has or because they have separated for a period of time that is taken to evidence this breakdown. 80/ In jurisdictions that follow the latter two models, any woman who wishes to divorce her husband for cruelty, be it physical, sexual or emotional, will have no difficulty in achieving her aim. Where the law fits the first paradigm, however, she may face difficulties.

Thus, for example, in a few jurisdictions, legislation will allow a woman to divorce her husband where he has changed his religion to that of Christianity and gone through a marriage with another woman; where he has been guilty of incestuous adultery, bigamy with adultery; marriage with another woman with adultery, rape, sodomy and bestiality or adultery coupled with desertion without reasonable cause for two years. 81/ Her husband, however, need only prove that his wife is guilty of adultery.

The fact that a woman who is the subject of domestic maltreatment may be able to proceed for divorce or judicial separation may be a hollow solution to her. First, legal separation and even divorce do not guarantee that the woman will be protected from violence. 82/ Secondly, many women who are the subject of domestic violence are not married or if they are married may not wish to separate from or divorce their husbands. Their priority is to end the vio- lence in their relationship, rather than the relationship itself. Further a victim may shun such relief out of shame, because divorce is culturally and socially unacceptable or in order to keep her family together or maintain her and her children's standard of living. Thirdly, even where she wants to end her marriage she may be faced with legal obstacles.

Except in those jurisdictions where divorce is available on assertion of breakdown or on proof of separation, she will have to show that grounds for divorce exist. Here the burden of proof is on her and she will have to carry this burden to the satisfaction of a judicial officer. This may be difficult if such an officer is dedicated to the concept of the sanctity of marriage or subscribes to the philosophy that a husband has the right to discipline his wife. In short, the marriage will not be dissolved if the judge is of the opinion that her circumstances do not indicate that her marriage should be brought to an end. 83/

In some countries, furthermore, couples who wish to divorce must attempt to reconcile before the courts will countenance an application for divorce. Thus, in Malaysia, for example, it is compulsory for couples to attend recon- ciliation where certain grounds for divorce are relied upon. 84/ A woman who has been the victim of abuse in such jurisdictions is in the unhappy position, in circumstances where she has decided to end her marriage, of having to meet with and attempt to agree with her attacker before her application is heard. Finally, in many countries the woman will have to await the elapse of a spe- cified period of time before she can proceed to divorce or separate from her husband. Effectively, this will keep her bound to the man unless she can prove her circumstances are exceptional for, in some situations, up to five years. 85/

B. Criminal law remedies

All forms of physical domestic violence and some forms of emotional abuse, such as threats of physical injury and demands for dowry, 86/ fall within the definition of criminal conduct. In most countries, therefore, except in so far as sexual crimes are concerned, a man is not entitled by reason of marriage or cohabitation to inflict violence upon his wife.

In principle, therefore, the criminal law may be invoked against a vio- lent spouse for common assault, assault occasioning actual bodily harm, assault occasioning grievous bodily harm, unlawful wounding, manslaughter, murder or any other criminal act. 87/ In various countries, also, new criminal legis- lation has been introduced to meet the challenge of certain objectionable conduct. Thus, for example, India and Bangladesh have passed statutes pro- viding severe criminal penalties for those who perpetrate violence in the context of dowry. In many countries, however, it is not a crime to rape or sexually assault a woman to whom one is married and from whom one is not legally separated. 88/

In practice, the criminal law has proved to be of little assistance to the victim of domestic violence. Traditionally the police have been blamed for the gap between the victim's abstract legal rights and her remedies in practice. So also have the courts, who have been criticized for their reluctance to view violence between spouses as a crime comparable to crime between strangers and for their willingness to accept the premise that traditional criminal law is inappropriate in the context of intimate relationships. These perceptions have led, it is believed, to easy bail and lenient sentences.

The appropriateness of the criminal justice system to and the role of the police in the context of family violence have already been canvassed, and the response of the courts and their personnel will be considered later. Here, however, it is appropriate to note that the criminal court is concerned primarily that the guilt of the offender should be established beyond reasonable doubt, and for this purpose cogent evidence must be adduced.

Crimes against intimates present serious evidentiary difficulties. As wife assault occurs usually in private circumstances, the victim will often be the only witness to the conduct and thus her evidence will be crucial to prove the guilt of the accused. Very often the victim will continue to live with or, at the very least, be in contact with her abuser until the criminal trial occurs. In such circumstances she is susceptible to threats and pleadings that seek to have her withdraw her complaint or fail to give evidence when the charge is heard.

It is commonly believed that wives withdraw criminal charges against their spouses, a view often offered as a justification for non-intervention by the criminal system into domestic violence (see page 56). While studies have indicated that withdrawal is a popular misconception (see page 56), change in prosecutorial policy can circumvent this problem. Thus, for exam- ple, in Canada, 89/ some of the states of Australia 90/ and the United States of America, 91/ police and prosecutors have been instructed to proceed with domestic violence cases as though they were cases between strangers, even in situations where the woman prefers the case to be dropped. 92/

In some countries wives cannot give evidence against their husbands in a criminal trial, while in others they may do so, but they need not if they do not wish to. In other words, wives are generally competent, but not compellable witnesses.

Where wives are incompetent to testify, evidence of domestic violence sufficient to convince a criminal court will be almost impossible to obtain. If the wife is competent, but not compellable, her husband may be able to convince her to refuse to testify. In a number of jurisdictions, legal provisions have been introduced to remove the issue of choice from a wife and put her in the same position as she would be if she were living with, but not married to, her husband or if she were any other individual and the crime were any other crime. Here, wives have been made compellable witnesses, although they may be excused if there are exceptional circumstances and they can show they have not been intimidated. 93/

Reforms of the nature of the pro-charging policy and compellability of spouses serve to remove some of the important technical difficulties that stand in the way of a successful criminal action. None the less, it is difficult to obtain a criminal conviction in any criminal case, a difficulty that is compounded in the context of domestic violence. Accordingly, many countries have sought other legal solutions for the problem of domestic violence and most have sought them in the civil law. In a number of Australian states, however, while criminal and civil law remedies have been resorted to, so also have quasi-criminal remedies, which are legal solutions that lie midway between the criminal and the civil law.

In many jurisdictions, summary courts are given the power to "bind over" any person to keep the peace or to be of good behaviour towards a particular person, in circumstances where the first person has been violent or threatened violence towards the second person. 94/ If the order is breached, the offender forfeits a specified sum of money or he may be imprisoned. Essentially the remedy lies between the criminal and the civil law. The process is criminal, but the standard of proof is lower.

In most countries the bind over is resorted to rarely. Certainly, in the context of domestic assault, it is inflexible, dilatory, has ineffective enforcement proceedings and is rarely enforced. 95/ In Australia, however, a legal process similar to the bind over has been especially tailored to confront violence in the home. Here, the police or a victim of domestic violence, which is widely defined to include incidents of harassment as well as physical abuse, can apply for an order to restrain the man when he has caused or threatened to cause personal injury or damage to property and unless restrained is likely to do so again. 96/

The man does not have to be present in court and the order is granted if it is shown that it is more probable than not that he caused or is about to cause the damage. Orders that can be made include forbidding the man to approach the woman and limiting his access to premises, even if he is the owner of the premises. If the order is breached, the man may be arrested without warrant and he is liable to be fined heavily or imprisoned. 97/

From a theoretical perspective, these orders would appear to have great potential to protect victims of domestic violence. From a practical, perspective, however, the response to them has been mixed. To a great extent, their usefulness depends on the police and their willingness to implement the procedures. In one Australian jurisdiction, the police have been quick to see the potential of the order and are vigorous in their pursuit of it, 98/ while in another, the police have not been so helpful. 99/ Again, police response can be best assured by training (see page 62) and involving the police at the very outset in an initiative. 100/ Victims have tended to view the orders negatively, 101/ while legal and welfare workers are more positive. 102/ However, despite this mixed response, no jurisdiction has sought to dismantle the legislation. Indeed, at present, New South Wales is strengthening and extending the availability of the order beyond spouses to those who share or have shared a common residence with the harasser or attacker, thus acknowledging the fact that siblings, parents and others in intimate relationships may be the subject of abuse. 103/ Further, New South Wales is issuing clear policy guidelines to the police initiating better training programmes.

C. Civil law remedies

Law reformers in many countries have responded to the general concern with violence against women in the home by improving civil remedies, rather than criminal remedies. Most legal systems provide an aggrieved person with personal remedies at civil law for any wrong that has been done to her or him. Thus, if a person is assaulted by another she or he can proceed against the attacker at civil law, in tort or delict, for monetary compensation. In principle, therefore, a wife should be able to bring an action in tort or delict against a husband who has performed a civil wrong against her. However, in many systems, the wife is denied this right.

In some countries women are considered to be perpetual minors and must sue under the guardianship of a man, their father or brother, if they are unmarried, or their husband, if they are married. 104/ This effectively serves to block off any compensation claim in the context of domestic violence for such women. In other systems, while women are fully competent to bring legal actions, they are denied the right of bringing actions against their husbands, on the basis that husband and wife are one and to sue each other would be to sue oneself. Even in those systems that allow such a suit, actions of this nature may normally be stopped by the court if no benefit is seen to arise from the litigation. 105/

Apart from the difficulties thus presented, it is questionable whether much benefit can be gained by suing in tort where domestic violence is concerned. The object of such an action is financial compensation that must be provided by the defendant. There is no therapeutic or punitive aspect to the action. Thus, it would appear that unless the defendant was possessed of financial resources and these resources were independent of the resources used to maintain the woman or the rest of the family, there would be little to gain from such an action as, in general terms, it would serve only to reduce the finances available to maintain the family. 106/

The civil law in most legal systems provides a remedy that is variously called an interdict or an injunction, a device that can be granted to support a primary cause of action.

Thus, for example, an injunction or interdict can be granted to stop the sale of a house, the ownership of which is in dispute. In the context of domestic violence, for example, such an injunctive remedy could be granted incidental or ancillary or proceedings for matrimonial relief, divorce or judicial separation, or in proceedings for delict or tort, to stop a husband from seeing his wife.

In many countries, an injunction or interdict of this nature can only be awarded in this incidental fashion. In other words it is not possible for a woman to get a court order to prevent her spouse molesting or harassing her unless she also applies for some form of primary or principal relief, such as a divorce, or if she sues him for a civil wrong. Thus, in these countries, while an order preventing the spouse from interfering with his wife can be given by the courts, the availability of the remedy will not provide her with any protection in circumstances where she is unable or does not wish to apply for matrimonial relief or a civil action. 107/

In some jurisdictions, however, law reformers have come to appreciate the potential of the injunction or interdict as a protective measure in the context of wife assault and special procedures have been introduced so that injunctive relief is available to a woman independently of any other legal action. 108/ Naturally, the remedies that have been introduced in the jurisdictions differ in detail. None the less, they do display similar characteristics that can be described and discussed.

In general terms, two sorts of orders can be given to the woman by the court. The first prohibits the man from harassing or molesting her, terms which have differing definitions, but usually include threats, constant following, phone-calls and contact. 109/ The second is more draconian and excludes the man from the home, even where it belongs to him. 110/ The orders are usually supported by a provision which allows the police to arrest the man if he breaches them. 111/ Penalties on arrest are also various, but the ultimate is imprisonment. 112/

The aim of the injunction procedures is to provide women with a short-term measure falling short of a criminal sanction where they are potential victims or victims of domestic assault, and the remedy has a number of advantages in the area of domestic assault. It indicates unequivocally to abusers that their behaviour is unacceptable and usually provides the police with effective power to act when violence reoccurs. 113/ Further, the legislation which provides such remedies usually allows them to be applied for in the absence of the attacker and in an expedited fashion. 114/

While the philosophy behind the legislation is laudable, the legislation and its implementation are not without difficulties. First, very often the remedies are limited by the statutes which authorize them. Some countries limit the remedies to an incidental part of a primary claim, such as divorce or delict and some countries bar certain groups of women from the remedies. 115/

In others, the statutory definition of abuse often omits psychological abuse or sexual violation. Again, the statute may limit access by confining the required relationship between the plaintiff and the defendant to, for example, husband and wife, thereby omitting former spouses or cohabitors or other relationships where abuse may occur. 116/ The procedures required may limit access. There may be a court filing fee and the remedy may require a degree of legal expertise that most lay people do not have, thus making it essential that the woman receive legal assistance. Here she may confront further difficulties because legal assistance may be scarce, or if available, lawyers may not be aware of the remedies 117/ or be expensive. Legal aid may not be available in the particular jurisdiction, or if it is, the woman may be disqualified from it because her eligibility may depend on the level of her husband's income. Further, sanction procedures may not be clear or strong enough. In short, the remedies may be deprived of their usefulness because they are introduced without attention to practical policy issues.

Ultimately, however, the effectiveness of protective injunctions, like all other legal remedies in the context of domestic violence, depends on the co-operation of the official actors involved. Here, again, the responses of the police and the judiciary are critical. Thus, in England and Wales, for example, where complex, but extremely comprehensive legislation exists to provide a woman with protection, (see page 70) the response of the police and judicial interpretation has weakened the potential for protection provided by the scheme. Police are often unaware of the existence of the protection order and reluctant to intervene if they know of it. 118/ Similarly, judges and magistrates have been loath to exclude a man from his home unless there is evidence of severe violence (see pages 71-72).

D. Conclusion

In many countries laws to protect women who are the subject of abuse are technically in place. However, at every level, the implementation of the law is fettered by the attitudes of those involved in the legal system: the police, prosecutors and the adjudicators. Throughout the system, there is a reluctance to intervene in the family unit, a reluctance that again reflects the twin ideologies of the sanctity and the privacy of the family.

Prosecutors 119/ like police (see page 57) tend to view their role in cases of domestic violence as one of mediation rather than prosecution, and thus they will often seek to pressurize a woman into dropping her complaint or they will attempt to divert her case to a civil or family court.

To a large extent, also, the protection of women depends on the reaction of judges. Judges have the ultimate legal authority in the criminal justice system. If they listen too uncritically to pleas of provocation based on "flightiness" or "nagging" or trivialize family violence by sentencing lightly, they reinforce dominant ideologies and the victim will receive neither justice nor protection. The individual man will perceive his behaviour as insignificant and he will continue to abuse, while the wider community will also continue to view domestic crime as acceptable. 120/

The effectiveness of any innovative legislative response is also dependent on the attitude of the judiciary. Very often legislation is open to differing interpretations and judges may be extremely reluctant to exercise a discretion in the absence of clear guidelines. Here the experience of England and Wales, where one of the first statutes providing orders to prohibit the man molesting the woman and excluding him from the home was introduced in 1976, is particularly instructive. Here the legislation was widely worded and allowed for judicial interpretation. Initially, judicial response was sympathetic, 121/ but later interpretation was coloured by attitudes towards the family, the position of the woman as a mother and the property rights of the man. 122/

Effective legal response is dependent, therefore, on all levels of the legal system, from the police to the judiciary, responding effectively to the issue. Their current failure to respond adequately stems from a combination of factors.

In the main, all levels of the legal system are ignorant of the dynamics of wife assault 123/ and all adhere, albeit in some cases unconsciously, to traditional values that support the family and the dominance of the male party within it. Thus, for example, commentators have suggested that judges are "unable to break out of the traditional belief that the family is a sacrosanct unit vital for healthy society. Conciliation is a court's primary aim". 124/

Further, members of the legal system face frustration because of the disposition of cases at other levels of the system. Thus, an arresting officer will face disillusionment if a prosecutor fails to press charges against a man, while the prosecutor will also be frustrated if she or he prosecutes and the defendant is acquitted on a technicality or, if convicted, receives only a nominal sanction. While much of this frustration is the result of the fact that very often the approach to wife abuse is incoherent and is not interrelated, some arises from the fact that the sentencing options available to justices at the end of the process appear inadequate.

To many judges, the traditional punitive response of the criminal justice system appears totally inappropriate to cases of domestic crime. Both imprisonment and fines will affect not only the abuser, but the victim and her entire family. Thus, sentences imposed are usually extremely lenient, with the husband, in most cases, being absolutely or conditionally discharged or released on probation. Fines are occasionally levied, but incarceration is rare.

Because of this, and to relieve pressure from over-crowded courts, diversion or mediation schemes, which defer or suspend prosecution if the man agrees to enter into a mediation/conciliation process with his wife so that they can reach a voluntary and mutually satisfactory agreement, have been advocated. Typically, such schemes require the man to enter into a programme of counselling.

Diversion occurs before any adjudication of guilt and, in the schemes that presently exist, divert the man from the criminal process at one of two stages: at the time when an arrest would normally have been made, thus being police-initiated; or prior to trial, at the behest of the prosecutor.

The schemes are based on the premise that families should be protected from the intrusiveness of the justice system and that problems within families are best solved through informal remedies that help the parties communicate more effectively, 125/ and are attractive because they promise a more humane approach to domestic violence than the traditional criminal justice system. The schemes are not, however, totally unproblematic, and have received serious criticism.

The schemes place the parties on an equal footing and ask them to negotiate an agreement for future behaviour. This dynamic means that the assailant is not punished for his crime and, indeed, it suggests that his victim shares responsibility for his actions. She is required to modify her behaviour in exchange for his promise not to abuse her further. The seriousness of wife abuse is, thus, not acknowledged and its nature is misconceived. Furthermore, any agreement that arises out of the mediation or conciliation is voluntary and unenforceable and thus the woman is given no guarantee that she will be protected from further violence.

The forum in which such agreements are reached tends to be inadequate. Most hearings are conducted in private, no records are kept, or if they are, such are generally confidential, thus protecting the process from public accountability. 126/ Both parties are usually present, representation is rarely allowed or, if allowed, parties generally fail to take advantage of their right. Hearings are frequently short and mediators are of varying competence, some being professionals, whereas others are minimally trained volunteers. 127/ Some cases are mediated without reference to the violence, many abused women being loath to raise the issue in front of their husbands. 128/

Perhaps the most important drawback of these schemes is that they cater more directly to the needs and desires of the abuser than those of his victim. He has the most to gain from a satisfactory settlement and will therefore appear co-operative. She may acquiesce in the settlement because of her unequal position, both in the relationship and in the mediation. She will thus suffer victimization, receiving the message that society considers the abuse trivial, while her spouse is subtly informed that he can get away with his actions. 129/

Diversion schemes, thus, present difficulties. This is not to say, however, that all approaches to domestic abuse based on mediation and conciliation are necessarily counter-productive or necessarily implicate the woman in the abuse. Thus, in certain societies, where mediation and conciliation are part of the cultural structure, such mediation and conciliation can be as effective a sanction to the man as arrest and conviction. Thus, for example, the intervention of the "neighbourhood committee" or the "habitant group" in China 130/ or the Village Court in Papua New Guinea 131/ or conciliators in African countries 132/ may be enough to show the man that his violence is unacceptable and should not be repeated. No matter what system is used, the essential factor is that the man must be shown to be responsible for his actions and the woman must be absolved from blame. In most systems, conviction following arrest and prosecution seems to give the clearest message: such conviction indicates the seriousness of the offence and also provides protection and support for the victim.

Sentencing on conviction need not, however, be confined to traditional punitive options, incarceration and fines, but can, for example, provide for weekend or evening incarceration, and also incorporate effective treatment for the abuser. Unlike in the case of diversion schemes, where a condition that the abuser attend for treatment is often stipulated, where such is a part of a conviction, attendance can be enforced. 133/

It is important, finally, that women are provided with legal avenues to counter abuse. These legal avenues should be as adequate as possible and the agencies involved in their implementation should act in all good faith.

Legal remedies alone, however, are insufficient. If the law is to be used to its best advantage there must be a change in attitude to family violence, which can be brought about most effectively by a clear commitment from Governments who must ensure that adequate resources are available to provide for abused women, that education and training schemes for all those involved in the system are introduced and that public educational measures to raise the general level of awareness of domestic violence are initiated. Women and men in the community must be well-informed on domestic violence, the conduct must be clearly condemned and the strategies available to deal with its occurrence well-publizised and easily accessible. Further, legal strategies must be well co-ordinated with other support systems for the abused woman. Thus, the health, welfare and community sector response must be appropriate, and inter-relate and co-ordinate both with each other and with the justice system.

IV. RESPONSE OF THE HEALTH, WELFARE AND COMMUNITY SECTORS

Although strategies to assist abused women have been seen primarily in terms of the law, the view being that it is critically important that appropriate legal provisions exist so that the abused woman has a framework of legal rights and that there should be no gap between these formal rights and rights in practice, it is essential that it is appreciated that legal change alone will not prevent violence against women in the family, nor necessarily protect a woman at risk.

In practice, the law is the last resort for women who are the victims of abuse. The pattern of help-seeking of such victims is fairly similar. First, informal sources of help, such as family or friends, are approached. Then, perhaps, more formal avenues, for example, a priest or pastor. Then, help may be sought from nurses, doctors and social workers. It will only be finally, usually when the abuse is very serious and frequent, that the police and lawyers are involved. 134/

Given this pattern of help-seeking, it is important to examine the response of individuals who may come in contact with women who are abused within their families. As the first outside contact is usually the doctor, 135/ this chapter will begin with an examination of the response of the health sector. This will be followed by a perusal of the response of the welfare sector. The community response will then be examined, concentrating on the shelter movement and "battering men's" programmes.

A. The response of the health sector

While the available evidence suggests that the medical practitioner will be the first formal source of help that a victim of spouse abuse will approach, the response of doctors has, in the main, proved to be unsatisfactory.

In general, the medical profession is not informed on the nature and magnitude of the problem, and women who present themselves with symptoms are very often misdiagnosed. Women often do not tell the doctor that they are abused, but will complain of depression, anxiety and vague somatic complaints. 136/ Even in cases where it is clear that they have sustained physical injury, doctors misdiagnose, accepting the woman's fictitious account of how she sustained the injury, which she will produce because she is ashamed or fearful of wasting the doctor's time. 137/ Doctors, who may suspect that the woman's story is untrue and that she is a victim of abuse, may prefer not to inquire too closely, perhaps because they do not wish to become involved in marital conflict. 138/ As the Dobashes point out:

"The doctor's failure to question the woman about the injuries or his willingness to accept a clear fabrication concerning the cause of the injury results in a mutual denial of the violence leading to it." 138/

In those cases where the doctor has been forced to confront the fact that the woman has been abused, response has tended also to be inadequate. Stark and her colleagues have documented the approach of the American medical professional which they see as exacerbating, rather than relieving the problem. 139/ They found that the battering was ignored, while the complaints associated with the abuse were treated symptomatically. Thus, they discovered, that at first, their physical trauma were treated as legitimate medical problems, but as the women reappeared for treatment, the doctors would reassess the problem and see the abuse as symptomatic of a particular social

or psychopathological problem. The diagnosis then shifted and its focus
became not the abuse or the abuser, but the woman, who was then labelled as an
alcoholic, a drug abuser, an hysteric or a depressive. The woman was then
prescribed antidepressants or was sometimes diagnosed, and thus disposed of,
as seriously psychiatrically disturbed. 139/

The medical profession has, thus, where it has recognized the abuse, seen
it as a problem requiring local solutions. In general terms, the abuse of the
woman is not addressed. She is rarely referred to social service agencies or
any form of supportive organization. Most often, she is prescribed drugs that
are inappropriate and may be harmful. The abuse is seen to be the woman's
problem, rather than that of her batterer. In cases where she is believed,
and not seen as an hysterical lier, 140/ the issue has been seen in psychiatric
terms: she is seen as frigid, masochistic, masculine, castrating, controlling
and aggressive, and often blamed because she is believed to have sought out a
violent mate and situation that she enjoys. 141/

The inadequate response of the medical profession is due to perspectives
doctors have towards wife abuse. With the rest of the helping professions,
doctors are of the opinion that the maintenance of the family unit is an
important goal. Moreoever, they very often do not see treatment of marital
problems of their patients as constituting "real medicine", real medicine constituting diagnosis and treatment of illness and injury. 142/ Much of this
stems from current medical training, which stresses individual case history
and pathology, rather than an holistic approach. Medical students are taught
to treat an individual's symptoms, not an experience or a situation.

While the inadequate response of the medical profession to wife abuse can
be explained, inappropriate response reinforces the woman's victimization and
thus must be ameliorated. This will occur only through education and training
of the profession at undergraduate and postgraduate levels and through refresher
programmes. Student doctors must be made aware of the pervasiveness and dynamics of family violence and must be taught to ask appropriate questions of
patients in situations where abuse may be occurring. 143/ Medical training
should move towards a more holistic approach to treatment - an approach which
is now being taken in a number of countries. 144/ Refresher programmes to
inform doctors of the problem should be initiated, the issue must be addressed
in professional and academic journals and protocols should be developed and
implemented for use in hospitals and doctors' surgeries, which assist in the
identification of abuse and the appropriate treatment for battered women. 144/

B. The welfare sector

The response of the medical profession to the issue of wife abuse is
typical of the more general neglect of maltreatment throughout the helping
services. Like medical practitioners, social and community workers have
continued to see abuse as a private event within a family brought about by
alcoholism or psychopathology.

Social and community workers have not responded to the specific problems
of the battered woman and her children with the sensitivity and patience that
the issue requires. Many are unaware of the complexities and ramifications of
the problem. Particulary, such professionals are unaware of the ambivalence
that an abused woman may feel, for example, they may find it difficult to
understand why a victim of abuse will not immediately leave her husband.

The welfare sector tends to be committed to a traditional view of the family and thus emphasizes its maintenance and reconciliation. 145/ Further, welfare professionals are very likely to see the problem as one of child care, thereby rendering the woman's problem marginal. 146/ Moreover, studies reveal that assumptions concerning the woman's role in the family very often lead social workers to offer women who are the victims of abuse little positive support. Thus, Maynard, who analysed 109 social work files in the United Kingdom, discovered the following four factors. First, any housewifely or wifely deviation was regarded as evidence of the woman's inadequacy, and her inability to cope and perform her duties properly, so that the breakdown in the family became the woman's private problem that she must rectify. Secondly, there was a reluctance to believe what the woman said about her situation. Thirdly, tacit support for the nuclear family and the inferior status of the woman within it was revealed. This led to an obsession with the restoration of the domestic equilibrium, even though the battering was still occurring and the status quo was obviously detrimental to the woman. Finally, there was tacit support for male domination and control of women by the fact that reasons for violence were implicitly supported and women were encouraged to understand and respond to these reasons. 147/

The response of the welfare sector can again be attributed to current patterns of training. The issue itself is not part of traditional training, the problems of children and child abuse are regarded as priorities and workers are taught to work with "families" and to seek solutions within the family context. 148/

The welfare sector is a critical sector and could be used to good effect within the context of the problem of wife abuse. Social and welfare workers are in a focal position and are equipped to provide information on the law and law enforcement sectors, the process and procedures for financial and other support offered by the State and can refer to appropriate professionals who are able to provide supportive counselling.

Again, training is critical, as are prepared protocols for those who are already in practice. It is very important where this training is concerned, however, that they are made aware that the woman herself must make the decisions. They must be sensitized to the fact that it may take some time for a battered woman to decide whether she will leave her spouse or remain with him. They must be aware that this ambivalence is not necessarily a sign of weakness, but indicative only of the fact that each woman is different and will make her decision at a different time from another woman.

C. Shelters

The leaders in the attempt to break through society's indifference to wife abuse, and to provide relief for the victims of the conduct, have been women's groups who spearheaded the shelter movement.

The first shelter for battered women was established in 1971 in England. It was initially conceived of as an advice centre for women with troubled marriages, but soon broadened to provide residential accommodation. In the years that have followed the establishment of this shelter, the shelter movement has become international, so that now, for example, there are over 700 shelters in the United States and shelters exist in such varied countries as Egypt, Thailand and Trinidad and Tobago. However, although the movement is international, shelters do not exist in every country in the world and often where they do exist they are overcrowded, not funded or underfunded and staffed by unpaid volunteers.

The shelter movement has had two effects. First, and most importantly, it has provided a haven for women who are abused, and secondly, it has drawn attention to the fact that wife assault is a real social problem. The movement is not, however, without its critics. Some argue that refuges speed the breakdown of marriages. This criticism is not supported by the research, which indicates that the refuge is a place of last resort and that women will exhaust all mechanisms of informal support and only then turn to the refuge. Indeed, women who use such facilities are very often socially isolated and live a long distance from relatives. Moreover, research reveals that the women who attend the refuge are very frequently at the end of their marriages. They may return to their husbands, but they will usually eventually leave them. The evidence is, therefore, that women will use a refuge or shelter when their marriage is ending, but the end may be slow and painful. 149/

There is little systematic research to date into the functioning of shelters or the impact of shelters on an abusive relationship. 150/ Further, there is very little information on what happens to victims after they leave the shelter. One recent study 150/ does, however, suggest that shelters do have beneficial effects on violent households, but that this might be dependent upon the attributes of the victim. If the woman is seen as actively taking control of her life, a shelter stay may dramatically reduce the likelihood of further abuse, but in other situations, the shelter stay may have no impact and, indeed, may even trigger new violence. 150/

It is clear that further research into the impact of shelters in the context of abuse is a priority. It seems, however, that women who are abused must have somewhere to go that is safe. This does not have to be an orthodox shelter or refuge, but advantage could be taken of safe places that may exist within the cultural context. Again, the safe place must fit in with the cultural context and not be a slavish adaptation of current shelter systems that may exist elsewhere.

A refuge can be many things for many women. It provides survival, safety, support, self-esteem and information. It can often amount to a turning point for a woman. Thus, Pahl, who twice interviewed a group of women who had used a refuge - once when they had just used it and again some years later - discovered that the refuge had been important to all the women. Many of the women knew they wanted to end their relationship before they got to the refuge but only found the ultimate courage to make the break after staying there, while others used it as a symbol to their husbands to indicate that the relationship would be at an end if the violence did not stop. 151/ All found the refuge to be a place where they could recover from their shame and isolation and where they gained support, help and friendship.

It is clear that without alternative accommodation, a woman is unable to make many decisions with regard to her relationship and thus some form of shelter system is crucial. Care must be taken, however, that the refuges are of a decent standard, well funded and well staffed. 152/ Protocols must take into account religious and cultural differences which may exist between residents, 153/ provision should be made for women with particular problems, for example, immigrant women and disabled women, 154/ and the refuge must provide access to services such as drug programmes and counselling. Further, assistance must be available to allow the woman to find more permanent accommodation and, perhaps, employment.

More importantly, shelters must operate on a confidential basis. 155/ It is critical that the location of the shelter should be kept as secret as possible and that protection should be available for its residents and staff.

In the main, such protection is or can be guaranteed most effectively if there is a close relationship between the shelters and the police, a practice that exists in, for example, Canada.

Again, the shelter or refuge should be seen as a component only of a co-ordinated and multifaceted programme. If this is not the case, the shelter programme may be used as an excuse to relieve other sectors of their responsibility in the combat of violence against women in the home.

D. Batterers' programmes

A number of programmes which aim to treat batterers have been established in the United States, Canada and Australia. 156/ Most of these programmes began as community-based responses to the problem and many were linked to the women's refuge in the community.

The rationale behind the programmes is laudable, their primary aim being to prevent recurrent violence, research revealing that recidivism is high both within the current relationship, if it is resumed, or within any succeeding relationship. The programmes also aim at addressing what is seen as a crucial factor underlying the poor response of the justice system to wife abuse: the paucity of sentencing options available once the man is convicted of an offence. The most common disposition is discharge or a suspended sentence, which, essentially, is no penalty. This discourages the police and the victim from pursuing charges and gives the appearance that the system and, by implication, society, tolerates the violence.

Gaol terms, although punitive and expressing abhorrence of the violence, present difficulties. Gaols are often overcrowded, place the man in an atmosphere that is conducive to the maintenance of his violence and frequently go against the wishes of the victim. Offender treatment, provided by "batterers' programmes" is thus the logical option, satisfying the justice system's desire for rehabilitation and the victim's goal of eliminating the violence in her relationship. In practice, offender treatment in such programmes is part of a diversion scheme (see page 72) or is part of the sentence meted out by the court.

Batterers' programmes are certainly justified on rational and moral grounds. A number of problems do confront them, however. First, they are, on the whole, voluntary and underfunded and are usually unevenly distributed in the community, being found primarily in major urban centres. 157/

Secondly, the clinical work in this area is new and formal training differs. The groups are modelled variously. Some use two counsellors, some one, some stress the gender of the counsellor, while others do not. Further, a range of psychotherapy skills and techniques are utilized. 158/

The most important and final problem that confronts the programmes is that there has been no well-designed analysis of the effectiveness of the treatment. Group leaders are confident that counselling works for at least some percentage of the men they see. However, most are unable to make conclusive generalizations about the overall effectiveness of the programmes. They are unable, apart from anecdotal reports, to indicate what sort of men are more amenable to such programmes or how long the changes last. 159/

It is important that the real effect of batterers' programmes is explored systematically. Anecdotal reports suggesting that the programmes effectively reduce abuse are insufficient. However, until it is shown that the programmes do more harm than good, there is no suggestion that they be dismantled or that new programmes should not be introduced.

E. Conclusion

The reponse of the health and welfare sectors of the community to the issue of wife abuse has, like the responses of all other sectors of society, been coloured by traditional beliefs that value the maintenance of the family and perpetuate the inferiority of the female partner to the man within the family unit. Health and welfare workers have preferred to remain unaware of spouse abuse, and when confronted with evidence of its occurrence have sought to find explanations for it in the conduct of the woman.

It is clear that education is the key to improvement of such response. The health and welfare professions must be educated in the dynamics of wife assault, they must be initiated into an holistic response to the problem and specifically trained against indicating to the woman that the problem is hers alone and of her own making. They must be trained to protect the woman and see her problem as important. Here, while the plight of her children may be important, it must not be emphasized to the extent that hers becomes marginalized and secondary. The woman must be protected and her dignity must be respected. While the maintenance of the family is important, the protection of women and respect for their basic human rights, fundamental freedom and dignity are equally important.

Grass-roots responses to family violence have been most effective in bringing the issue to public attention and providing safety, shelter and support for women at risk. Such responses must be supported and strengthened. It is critical, however, that such responses should be as adequate as possible. Research into their effectiveness is important, as is adequate funding and government support.

In the end analysis, however, no one response is sufficient. The response to violence against women in the home must be a co-ordinated, multifaceted and interrelated one. The issue is multi-dimensional and the response must be also.

Notes

1/   See, for example, article 8, European Convention on Human Rights (1). Everyone has the right to respect for his private and family life, his home and his correspondence. See also, International Covenant on Civil and Political Rights, 1966, article 17.

2/   This is subject to interference in the interests of national security, public safety or the economic well-being of the country, for the prevention of disorder or crime and for the protection of the rights and freedoms of others.

3/   Family privacy is particularly stressed in traditional societies: see, for example, with respect to Canadian aboriginals, Canadian Council on Social Development, Native Crime Victims Research (Ottawa, Department of Justice, 1984), p. 4.

4/   Mendez, Working Paper for Expert Group Meeting on Violence in the Family with Special Emphasis on its Effects on Women, December 1986.

5/   S. Maidment, "The relevance of the criminal law to domestic violence", Journal of Social Welfare Law, No. 26, 1980. S. Maidment, "The law's response to marital violence in England and the U.S.A.", ICLQ, 1977, p. 405.

6/   L.E.M. Mukasa-Kikonyogo, Ugandan case study (Kampala, High Court of Uganda) where the author states: "the social, economic and cultural background does not suit criminal and domestic laws envisaged and recommended by developed countries". L. A. Long, "Cultural considerations in the assessment and treatment of intrafamilial abuse", American Journal of Orthopsychiatry, No. 56, 1986, p. 131, which describes two cases of child abuse in traditional North American Indian clans. In both the informant was ostracized and harassed.

7/   A. Lazlo and T. Mclean, "Court diversion: an alternative for spousal abuse cases", in United States Commission on Civil Rights Consultation, Battered Wives: Issues of Public Police (Washington, DC, January 1978).

8/   M. Wilt and R. K. Breedlove, Domestic Violence and the Police: Studies in Detroit and Kansas City (Washington, DC, Police Foundation, 1977), p. 9.

9/   Mediation and counselling was recommended by the study.

10/   L. W. Sherman and R. A. Berk, "The specific deterrent effects of arrest for domestic assault", American Sociological Review, No. 49, 1984, p. 261.

11/   Ibid., p. 270.

12/   R. A. Berk and P. J. Newton, "Does arrest really deter wife battery? An effort to replicate the findings of the Minneapolis spouse abuse experiment", American Sociological Review, No. 50, 1985, p. 253.

13/   See, for example, Oregon in the United States of America: Or. Rev. Stat. 133.055 (2) 1981. Other States in the United States make arrest mandatory after a protection order has been breached: Wash. Rev. Code 26.50.110 (2) (Supp. 1984); Minn. Stat. Ann. 518B.01 914) (West Supp. 1984); N.C. Gen. Stat. 50B-4(b) (Supp. 1984); Wash. Rev. Code Ann 10.99.0303 (3) (a) (West Supp. 1985); Minn. Stat. Ann. 6299.341 subd. 1 (West Supp. 1984); N.C. Gen. Stat. 15A-401 (b) (3) (Supp. 1981); Del. Code Ann. tit. 13,1510 (Replacement vol. 1981).

14/   P. Jaffe and others, "The impact of the police laying charges in incidents of wife abuse", Journal of Family Violence, No. 1, 1986, p. 37. This study was particularly useful because of the existence of an earlier study wherein victim selection was identical in the same region, thereby allowing for pre and post policy victim perception. For the earlier study see P. Jaffe and C. A. Burris, An Integrated Response to Wife Battering: A Community Model, Research Report of the Solicitor General of Canada (1982).

15/   In many jurisdictions the person who has been victimized has the responsibility of bringing the charge. See, for example, Kuwait where article 109 of the Criminal Procedure Law provides that certain criminal cases shall be brought only on the claim of the person who has been victimized. These include abuses and assault and thus cases of domestic abuse and assault will only be considered if wives proceed. This is also the case in Chile. ISIS Internacional, case study (Santiago), p. 7.

16/   D. Wood, Canadian case study (Ottawa, Social Policy at Status of Women Canada, 1987), p. 12; and Federal/Provincial/Territorial Report on Wife Battering to the Meeting of Ministers Responsible for the Status of Women, Niagara on the Lake, 28-30 May 1984.

17/ H. L'Orange, case study from New South Wales (Sydney, Government Domestic Violence Committee, 1987).

18/ L. MacLeod, <u>Battered But Not Beaten</u> (Ottawa, Canadian Advisory Council on the Status of Women, 1987), p. 24.

19/ <u>Ibid.</u>, p. 87. See also, Wood, <u>op. cit</u>.

20/ Australian Law Reform Commission, <u>Domestic Violence</u>, Report No. 30, (Canberra, A.G.P.S., 1986), p. 14. See also L'Orange, <u>op. cit</u>.

21/ See Report of the Committee to Investigate the Response of the London Metropolitan Police Force into Domestic Violence, 1986, unpublished.

22/ Australian Law Reform Commission Report, <u>Domestic Violence</u> ..., p. 15.

23/ V. G. Binney and others, <u>Leaving Violent Men</u> (Women's Aid Federation, 1981).

24/ <u>Ibid.</u>, p. 15. See also, N. Oppenlander, "Coping or copping out", <u>Criminology</u>, No. 20, 1982, p. 449, who derived data from a data base of 596 police investigations of arguments and assaults from 5,688 officer/citizen encounters in 24 communities of Rochester, New York, Tampa, St. Petersburg, Florida and St. Louis, Missouri, which totalled 10% of all police calls. The author examined first the initial dispatch and then the discrepancy between this and the actual problem and discovered that the police were slower to arrive at domestic disputes and that the officers tended to mediate in cases of domestic violence, although they had no training. Similar results appear in D. Bell, "Domestic violence: victimisation, police intervention and disposition", <u>Journal of Criminal Justice</u>, No. 13, 1985, p. 425, in relation to domestic disputes and violence incidents in Ohio and in a study conducted by the Bedfordshire Police in the United Kingdom in 1976 and in the Report of the Committee to Investigate the Response of the London Metropolitan Police to Cases of Domestic Violence in 1986. Similarly, Susan Edwards research on police response to domestic violence in two districts of metropolitan London found that of 449 incidents reported to one police station in a six month period only 13% were officially recorded and of these only 11 or 2.4% were proceeded with. Of the 324 calls to the other station, only five were proceeded with.

25/ M. D. Pagelow, <u>Woman Battering: Victims and Their Experiences</u> (Beverly Hills, Sage, 1981). Pagelow questioned 350 women of whom 200 had called the police on at least one occasion and more than half said that they had asked to have their spouse arrested. Of 86 women who answered "what happened next?" 60% said that the police had failed to make an arrest, 24% said that he was arrested and released shortly thereafter, while only 15% reported that he was arrested and brought to trial.

26/ R. E. Dobash and R. Dobash, <u>Violence Against Wives: A Case Against the Patriarchy</u> (London, Open Books, 1980), pp. 207-208, Binney, <u>op. cit</u>. J. Pahl, "Police response to battered women", <u>Journal of Social Welfare Law</u>, November 1982, p. 337. R. I. Parnas, "The police response to domestic violence", <u>Wisconsin Law Review</u>, vol. 2, Fall, 1967, p. 914.

27/ R. E. Worden and A. A. Pollitz, "Police arrests in domestic disturbances: a further look", <u>Law and Society Review</u>, No. 18, 1984, p. 105. S. K. Berk and D. R. Loseke, "Handling family violence: situational determinants of police arrests in domestic disturbances", <u>Law and Society Review</u>, No. 15, 1981, p. 315.

28/ Dobash and Dobash, <u>Violence Against Wives ...</u>, p. 207.

29/ <u>Ibid</u>. Other important variables indicating arrest rather than mediation that appear in the research are when the woman tells the police that she
wants her husband arrested, when she alleges violence, when both are present
at the same time and when the police believe that they will be able to suc-
cessfully pursue a prosecution given the character of the evidence and the
likelihood that the wife may withdraw the allegation. See the sources cited
in notes 21, 22 and 23 and the Evidence of the Association of Chief Police
Officers of England Wales and Northern Ireland to the Select Committee on Violence in the Family, Cmnd. (London, HM Stationery Office, 1975), pp. 367-368,
and Parnas, <u>loc. cit</u>., p. 914.

30/ J. Pahl, ed., <u>Private Violence and Public Policy: The Needs of
Battered Women and the Response of the Public Services</u> (London, Routledge and
Kegan Paul, 1985), pp. 88-89.

31/ M. El Husseiny Zaalouk, case study from Egypt (Cairo, The National
Center for Social and Criminal Research, 1987), p. 8.

32/ S. Papachan, case study from Malaysia (Selangor, Women's Aid
Organisation, 1987).

33/ J. O. Akande, case study from Nigeria (Lagos, Lagos State University,
Faculty of Law, 1987), p. 12.

34/ S. Skrobanek, case study from Thailand (Bangkok, Women's Information
Centre, 1987), p. 14.

35/ C. D. Spinellis, case study from Greece (Athens, University of
Athens, Faculty of Law, 1987), p. 12.

36/ Parnas quotes a police training manual: "many disturbance calls
require the services of the beat officer in settling quarrels and neighbourhood problems. These calls are often non-criminal in nature that do not
require arrest and in fact have no grounds on which to base legal arrest"
(Parnas, <u>loc. cit</u>., p. 919). See also, Dobash and Dobash, <u>Violence Against
Wives ...</u>, p. 210, and Susan Edwards unpublished interviews of 44 police
officers at two London police stations which revealed that most police officers disliked domestic disturbance work, many seeing such incidents as a
normal part of married life. See also, N. Johnson, "Police, social work and
medical response to battered women", in <u>Marital Violence</u>, N. Johnson, ed.,
Social Review Monograph No. 31 (London, Routledge and Kegan Paul, 1983),
p. 109; N. P. Simi, case study from Samoa (Apia, Prime Minister's Department)
and Akande, <u>op. cit</u>.

37/ Police often explain their reluctance to take a law enforcement role
in domestic disturbance cases as a result of the fact that most women withdraw
their allegations against their attacker on reflection and thus they are
unable to get convictions. For example, the Uganda case study indicates that
in most cases the woman will withdraw the initial complaint (Mukasa-Kikonyogo,
<u>op. cit</u>.). While certainly withdrawal by the woman will present the police
with severe practical difficulties in pursuing an action, recent research
indicates that there is no greater withdrawal in domestic violence cases than
in other actions. Report on Acts of Domestic Violence Committed in the Country
between 1 February and 31 July 1976 by the Bedfordshire Police Department in
the United Kingdom indicated that only 18 out of 104 cases of wife assault
were withdrawn. The Dobashes also found that only 6% of assault charges were

dropped and then only after considerable postponement of court proceedings (Dobash and Dobash, Violence Against Wives ...). Similarly, Wasoff in a study carried out in Scotland found that women who had been assaulted by their part-ners were no more likely than any other victim group to refise to press charges or withdraw charges once proceedings are initiated. F. Wasoff, "Legal protec-tion from wife-beating: the processing of domestic assaults by Scottish prosecutors and criminal courts", International Journal of the Sociology of Law, No. 10, 1982, p. 187. The perception that women withdraw charges is shared by police in Samoa, Uganda and Nigeria. See case studies by Simi, op. cit., Mukasa-Kikonyogo, op. cit., Akande, op. cit.

38/ See the research of Susan Edwards into two London police stations, 1986, unpublished, and the Report of the Committee to Investigate the London Metropolitan Police Force into Domestic Violence.

39/ R. Tong, Women, Sex and the Law (New Jersey, Rowman and Allanheld, 1984), p. 134, quotes the New York City Police Department Student's Guide which states that "family problems ... and non-criminal "disputes" or "distur-bances", essentially verbal in nature, not serious, and causing no one injury". See also, T. Faragher, "The police response to violence against women in the home", in Pahl, op. cit., p. 110, a report of a study into the Staffordshire County Police in England, who, the researcher found, saw domestic work as extraneous to "real" police work.

40/ See case studies by Papachan, op. cit., and by El Husseiny Zaalouk, op. cit., where police said it was the man's right.

41/ S. Atkins and B. Hoggett, Women and the Law (Oxford, Blackwells, 1984), p. 137, suggest that lighter sentences are imposed in cases of domestic violence compared with similar assaults in non-domestic circumstances and there is greater scope for defences such as provocation to be raised in the domestic context.

42/ This is guaranteed in many human rights instruments and many consti-tutions. See, for example, International Covenant on Civil and Political Rights, 1966, article 17.

43/ Australian Law Reform Commission, Domestic Violence ..., p. 15. See also Kuwaiti Criminal Procedure Law (1960) Arts. 48 and 54.

44/ Crimes Act 1900 (N.S.W.) s. 357F (2)-(3).

45/ Crimes Act 1900 (N.S.W.) s. 357F (4).

46/ Crimes Act 1900 (N.S.W.) s. 357G.

47/ The number of warrants issued in 1983 and 1984 was 6 in each year: New South Wales Domestic Violence Committee, Report April 1983 - June 1985 (Sydney, Government Printer, 1985), p. 20.

48/ The legislation in New South Wales requires such warrants to be issued by a judicial officer who must, herself or himself, be sure that there are reasonable grounds to suspect a domestic violence offence is about to occur, is occurring or has occurred. It also requires proper records of the warrants to be kept which include the address of the house, the name of the informant and details as to whether or when the house was entered after the warrant was issued.

49/ Australian Law Reform Commission, Domestic Violence ..., p. 18.

50/ Ibid. In many countries arrest is only allowed if proceedings by summons would not be "effective", a term which requires judicial interpretation.

51/ Donaldson v. Broomby (1981-82) 40 A.L.R. 525 per Deane J.

52/ Australian Law Reform Commission, Domestic Violence ..., p. 19, outlines the complications in the Australian Capital Territory one of the jurisdictions of Australia.

53/ Ibid., p. 20, para. 44.

54/ K. Waits, "The criminal justice system's response to battering: understanding the problem, forging the solutions", Washington Law Review, No. 60, 1985, pp. 267, 308. See also pages 107-108.

55/ For example, International Covenant on Civil and Political Rights, article 9.1: "Everyone has the right to liberty and security of person. No one should be subjected to arbitrary arrest or detention".

56/ Australian Law Reform Commission, Domestic Violence ..., p. 21, para. 46.

57/ See note 13.

58/ See notes 26 and 27. See also Pagelow, op. cit., p. 125, where she indicates that police particularly became disenchanted and followed a "peacekeeping" rather than "law enforcement" line when faced with violent relationships of long duration.

59/ Binney and others, op. cit., indicates that 35 of the women interviewed had some sort of order in place allowing the police to arrest, of these half called the police because of continuing violence but only 4 were charged with breaking the order and even where charged their punishment was light. See also Susan Edwards unpublished research (1986), wherein she reports that the police indicated that they had court orders that gave them authority to arrest if they saw it fit, but they said they rarely arrested even if the orders were breached.

60/ See note 37.

61/ 396 N.Y.S. 2d. 1974 (Sup. Ct. N.Y. County).

62/ P. W. Gee, "Ensuring police protection for battered women: the Scott v. Hart suit", Signs, No. 8, 1983, p. 554.

63/ Gee, loc. cit., indicates that this sort of approach can be successful as a campaign even if the plaintiffs do not succeed on the merits. It educates the public and law enforcement agencies about battered women's needs for effective criminal remedies and also puts pressure on agencies to change policies. In Oakland itself training programmes were introduced for police and large sums were given to shelter programmes and a Battered Women's Resource Card, explaining the legal rights of battered women and provides them with resource points, was designed to be carried by police and issued to women at risk.

64/ <u>Bail Act</u> 1978 (N.S.W.) s. 36-9.

65/ <u>Bail Act</u> 1978 (N.S.W.) s. 50.

66/ See note 24, and see the evidence of an officer to the Australian Law Reform Commission, "Yes, it's the worst job that we have to do. It's worse than deaths. You get used to them. But with domestics you can never do the right thing. The parties have had years of rotten marriage and you're there to try and do something about it. You know that whatever you do it's going to happen again. And in most cases you can't do anything anyway because the wife decides that she does not want to prosecute" (<u>Domestic Violence</u> ..., p. 26, para. 60).

67/ Police have the power to arrest at the outset and in most situations protection orders and interdicts include arrest powers for the police. See pages 69-70.

68/ See, for example, training in the United Kingdom which according to the Report of the Committee to Investigate the Response of the London Metropolitan Police to Cases of Domestic Violence in 1986 is informal, random and unstructured. Canada has introduced training for police on a more comprehensive basis; see Wood, <u>op. cit</u>.

69/ In Bogota, for example, training in domestic violence and rape cases is given to policewomen only. M. I. Plata, case study from Colombia (Bogota, PROFAMILIA-EEC-Population Concern), p. 23.

70/ See again the Report of the Committee to Investigate the Response of the London Metropolitan Police to Cases of Domestic Violence and Edwards, <u>op. cit</u>. This research into the response of two London police stations to incidents of domestic violence found that only a small percentage of cases reported were actually recorded.

71/ Such an initiative is about to be introduced in New South Wales, Australia. See New South Wales Government Violence against Women and Children Law Reform Task Force, Consultation Paper (New South Wales, Government Printer, July 1987), p. 88.

72/ See, for example, the Royal Canadian Mounted Police Rape Kit reproduced in <u>Confronting Violence: A Manual for Commonwealth Action</u>, Women and Development Programme (London, Commonwealth Secretariat, 1987).

73/ S. Pimentel, Brazilian case study, (São Paulo, Secretaria de Estado da Educaçao, Praça de República). Two such stations now exist in Santiago, Chile. ISIS Internacional, case study for Chile.

74/ L'Orange, <u>op. cit</u>. In Greece, also, the General Secretariat for Equality has sent a circular letter to all police stations in Greece outlining guidelines for accepting female victims of family violence, stating that "It is absolutely necessary to be understood by all members of the police force that females (as well as men), when they are victims of an offence, are citizens. For those citizens both police and legal protection should be operating to the highest possible degree. (This means) that women should not be considered under the spirit of a paternalistic, traditional attitude probably as a victim who is either partially or entirely guilty for the commission of the offence" (Spinellis, <u>op. cit</u>.).

75/ Malaysia, Islamic Family Law Acts (1985); Law Reform (Marriage and Divorce) Act (1982).

76/ See, for example, with regard to Africa, A. Phillips and H. P. Morris, Marriage Laws in Africa (Oxford University Press, 1971); T. W. Bennett and N. S. Peart, "The dualism of marriage laws in Africa", in Family Law in the Last Two Decades of the Twentieth Century, T. W. Bennett, ed. (Cape Town, Juta, 1983), p. 145.

77/ S. C. Bradley, "Attitudes and practices relating to marital violence among the Tolai of East New Britain", in Domestic Violence in Papua New Guinea, S. Toft. ed., Monograph No. 3 (Boroko, Law Reform Commission of Papua New Guinea, 1985), p. 34.

78/ See, for example, with respect to Zimbabwe, E. G. Bello, The Status of Women in Zimbabwe (Harare, 1985), pp. 12-14. See also, J. O. Akande, Law and the Status of Women in Nigeria U.N.: 1979. See also the sources in notes 76 and 77.

79/ See, for example, A. Ibrahim, Family Law in Malaysia and Singapore (Kuala Lumpur, 1978), pp. 206-222. For examples of legislation in countries where Islamic law has been codified and cruelty is provided as a ground for divorce, see, Administration of Muslim Law Act (Singapore) (Cap. 42) s. 49 and Islamic Family Law Acts (Malaysia) 1985, s. 52.

80/ An example of the first model is the Sierra Leone, Matrimonial Causes Act (Cap. 35), the second, England and Wales, Matrimonial Causes Act, 1973 and the third, Barbados, Family Law Act No. 29 of 1981.

81/ Divorce Act (Uganda) 1964, s. 5. Evidence exists to indicate that informal separation is far more common in Uganda than formal divorce proceedings, a fact which is not surprising given the grounds for divorce. See L.E.M. Mukasa-Kikonyogo, presentation delivered at the International Federation of Women Lawyers, Sydney, 26-31 August 1984. In Uganda there are rarely more than 100 petitions to the High Court each year.

82/ "Of those who never returned to the man .. 44% reported at least one violence incident with the man" (J. Giles-Sims, Wife Battering: A Systems Theory Approach (New York, Guilford Press, 1983), p. 138. See also MacLeod, op. cit., p. 28.

83/ This might be particularly problematic in jurisdictions where physical chastisement of a wife is enshrined in the law or accepted culturally. See, for example, Nigeria, where s. 55 (1) d of the Northern Nigerian Criminal Code justifies a "reasonable amount" of physical chastisement of a wife. See also Atkins and Hoggett, op. cit., p. 127, which cites a number of English cases where divorce was disallowed although the wife was the subject of cruelty. Note, further, the Egyptian case study, which reports a case where the court allowed wife battery because of religion (El Husseiny, op. cit.).

84/ Law Reform (Marriage and Divorce) Act, 1982, s. 103.

85/ Malaysia, for example, bars divorce unless there are exceptional circumstances until the marriage has lasted two years. Law Reform (Marriage and Divorce) Act 1982, ss. 53 and 54; Trinidad and Tobago for five years, unless there are exceptional circumstances: Matrimonial Proceedings and Property Act Cap. 45:51. In England and Wales the bar is absolute and is one year: Matrimonial Causes Act 1973, s. 3(1).

86/   See H. Singh, case studies for India (New Dehli, Ministry of Welfare, National Institute of Social Defence and Bangladesh), I. Shamim (Dhaka, University of Dhaka, Department of Sociology), and Dowry Prohibition Act (India) 1961 as amended and Dowry Prohibition Act (Bangladesh) No. XXXV of 1980 as amended and also Criminal Law (Second Amendment) Act (India) 1983. The latter legislation created a new offence of cruelty to a woman by her husband or the relatives of her husband. Cruelty is defined as any wilful conduct which is of such a nature as is likely to drive the woman to commit suicide or to cause grave injury to life or limb or health, whether physical or mental, of the woman. Cruelty also encompasses harassment of the woman where it is intended to coerce her or any of her relatives into parting with any property or valuable security or any harassment which occurs because of her failure or that of her relatives to meet such a demand.

87/   The statutes are different in each jurisdiction. Most do not, however, provide for the specific crime of wife abuse, but allow for prosecution of such an offence under the general statutory scheme. Examples of statutes are: Nigeria, Criminal Code, ss. 351-360, Penal Code, s. 262-265; Egypt, Penal Code No. 58 of 1937, Articles 240-243; Greece, Code of Criminal Procedure, Criminal Code; Kuwait, Criminal Law of 1960, Articles 161ff; Chile, Penal Code, Articles 397ff; Poland, Chapter XXV, Penal Code, 1969, Article 184 specifically refers to abuse within the family. Many of the statutory provisions are outlined in the case studies.

88/   Rape or sexual assault in marriage is a crime in only a very few jurisdictions: see U.S.S.R., Article 117, Criminal Code (1960); Czechoslovakia, s. 238, Criminal Code, 1950; Poland, Article 204, Criminal Code, 1932; Denmark, Criminal Code, 1960, ss. 216, 217, 218; Norway, Penal Code, 1902, s. 222; Sweden, Criminal Code, Ch. 6, s.1; Trinidad and Tobago, New Offences Act, 1986, s. 6 and see Case Study, prepared by K. N. Pryce, Senior Lecturer in Sociology, The University of the West Indies, St. Augustine, for history of the passage of the act; New Zealand, Crimes Amendment Act (No. 3) 1985, s. 2; Canada, Criminal Code, s. 246.8; Scotland, Forte (1983) 99 L.Q.R. 513; most Australian states and some states of America, The Marital Rape Exemption (1977) 52 N.Y.U.L. Rev. 306.

89/   P. Jaffe and C. A. Burris, "Wife abuse as a crime: the impact of police laying charges", Canadian Journal of Criminology, No. 25, 1983. See also pages 53-54.

90/   See pages 53-54 and case study from New South Wales (L'Orange, op. cit.).

91/   See pages 53-54 and case study from the United States of America (L. H. Herrington, former Assistant Attorney-General).

92/   See pages 53-54 and case study. Note, the United Kingdom will not be following the charging model. H. Mason, "Who keeps the peace", Sunday Times, 16 August 1987.

93/   Police and Criminal Evidence Act (U.K.) 1984, s. 80; Evidence Act (Canada), R.S.C. 1970, Ch. E-10, s. 4; Crimes Act 1900 (N.S.W.) s. 407AA. In some ways judicial officers have undermined the provision by allowing many women to escape from the compulsion. N.S.W. Domestic Violence Committee, Report April 1983 to June 1985 (Sydney, N.S.W. Government Printer), pp. 31-32. Note, in this context, the difficulty that has arisen in Canada where women have been imprisoned for contempt for refusing to give evidence against their abusive spouses. MacLeod, op. cit., p. 87, and Canadian case study (Wood, op. cit.)

94/ See, for example, Scotland: "law burrows", Canada: Criminal Code, R.S.C., 1970, s. 745; Hawkins, Pleas of the Crown, Book 1, ch. 60.

95/ Australian Law Reform Commission, Domestic Violence ..., p. 38.

96/ Justices Act 1921 (South Australia) s. 99; Justices Act 1902 (Western Australia) ss. 172, 173, 174; Peace and Good Behaviour Act 1982 (Queensland); Crimes Act 1900 (New South Wales) s. 547AA; Crimes (Domestic Violence) Ordinance 1986 (Australian Capital Territory). The details of the various pieces of legislation vary slightly.

97/ Ibid. See also New South Wales case study (L'Orange, op. cit.).

98/ South Australia: D. Naffin, Domestic Violence and the Law: A Study of s. 99 of the Justices Act (South Australia) (South Australia, Women's Adviser Office, June 1985), p. 127.

99/ N.S.W. Domestic Violence Committee Report, April 1983 to June 1985 (Sydney, Government Printer, 1985), p. 21.

100/ Australian Law Reform Commission, Domestic Violence ..., p. 48, and Naffin, op. cit., p. 94: "... whenever the police are committed, enthusiastic and conscientious, victims of domestic violence receive justice".

101/ Naffin, op. cit., p. 116.

102/ "According to this survey group the chief advantage of the orders is that they deter persons who are normally law-abiding from engaging in further acts of violence. To a limited extent, the orders are effective. The main problem with the orders - their principal disadvantage - is that they fail to deter persistent offenders who have developed cynical attitudes towards the law. It follows that the attitude of the respondent is all important. The extent to which the respondent takes the order seriously is the extent of its effectiveness" (Naffin, op. cit., p. 116).

103/ Violence Against Women and Children, Law Reform Task Force, Consultation paper (N.S.W., Government Printer, July 1987), pp. 80-88.

104/ This is the case with African women. R. Hirschon, ed., Women and Property, Women as Property (London, Croom Helm, 1984), Introduction. Note, however, this has been changed in Zimbabwe by Legal Age of Majority Act, 1982. See D. P. Galen, "Internal conflicts between customary law and general law in Zimbabwe: family law as a case study", Zimbabwe Law Review, No. 1, 1983, p. 3.

105/ See, for example, the England and Wales. Law Reform (Husband and Wife) Act, 1962. The court is allowed to stay proceedings if no substantial benefit would accrue to either party from the continuation of the proceedings.

106/ A number of countries provide government funded compensation schemes which provide financial remedies for those who have been the victims of criminal activity. Such a scheme is provided in the United Kingdom and entitled the Criminal Injuries Compensation Board. Such schemes often, however, limit their accessibility to battered women by stringently drawing their rules to exclude victims who are still living with their assailants and victims who fail to co-operate with the police. Indeed, some schemes of this nature exclude battered wives with a blanket exclusion of compensation for family violence.

107/   See, for example, Malaysia: <u>Law Reform (Marriage and Divorce) Act</u>
1982, s. 103. In Malaysia there is the added complication of compulsory counselling where the woman wishes to be divorced. Moreover, the legislation does
not apply to Muslim and aboriginal women.

108/   The jurisdictions that provide such relief include a number of the
U.S. states: for example, <u>Abuse Prevention Act</u>, Massachusets General Laws,
Chap. 209A; Australia, <u>Family Law Act</u> 1975 (Cth.) s. 114; Malaysia, supra note
134a; Singapore, <u>Women's Charter</u> s. 65A; Hong Kong, <u>Domestic Violence Order</u>,
1986; a number of the Canadian states, <u>Family Law Reform Act</u>, R.S.O. 1980
(Ontario) c. 152, s. 45, <u>Matrimonial Property Act</u>, 1980 (Nova Scotia) c. 9,
s. 12, <u>Family Law Reform Act</u> (Prince Edward Island) s. 34; New Zealand,
<u>Domestic Protection Act</u> 1982; United Kingdom, <u>Matrimonial Homes Act</u> 1983
(England and Wales), <u>Domestic Proceedings and Magistrates' Courts Act</u> 1978
(England and Wales) s. 18, <u>Domestic Violence and Matrimonial Proceedings Act</u>
1976 (England and Wales), <u>Matrimonial Homes (Family Protection) Act</u> 1981
(Scotland), <u>Domestic Protection Order (Northern Ireland)</u> 1980 and St. Vincent
and Grenadines.

109/   Usually such behaviour is open to judicial interpretation. In
Australia, for example, such a remedy was granted to prevent the mental
violence of insulting and denigrating the victim in front of the couple's
children: <u>Plows and Plows</u> (1979) FLC 90-712, while in England such was
awarded in one case to stop the husband calling at the wife's house and at
her place of work: <u>Vaughan</u> v. <u>Vaughan</u> (1973) 1 W.L.R. 1159.

110/   See legislation cited in note 108.

111/   The legislation again differs here. In some cases a power to arrest
is automatically attached to the injunction or interdict - see, for example,
Scotland - in others this is a matter for judicial discretion - see, for
example, England and Wales - or if the victim asks for it - see, for example,
Australia. New Zealand's provision is novel. If the man breaches an order he
is arrested and compulsorily imprisoned for 24 hours. This latter provision
has been criticized for being a violation of natural justice in that the
offender is denied the right to appear before an adjudicatory body and thus
brands the man with guilt before trial. See Atkin and others, "Protecting the
victims of domestic violence - the Domestic Protection Act", <u>Victoria
University Law Review</u>, No. 14, 1984, p. 119.

112/   See legislation cited in note 108.

113/   Pahl, <u>op. cit.</u>, p. 89.

114/   See legislation cited in note 108. Some statutes provide for
expedited orders and ex parte orders, whereas some do not.

115/   See note 108.

116/   Incidents of abuse often occur amongst former couples: see, for
example, the Report of the New South Wales Domestic Violence Committee to the
Premier of New South Wales, Government Printer, N.S.W.: September 1985 at
p. 35 where it is noted that courts are extremely reluctant to consider sus-
pension or denial of access to violent fathers and maintain a distinction
between matters concerning the protection of the woman and matters concerning
the welfare of the children. Indeed, the Report, indicates, much violence,
abuse, harassment and intimidation accompanies access visits. Figures from
Australia indicate that in 64.3% of the cases of domestic assault, the offender
and the complainant are no longer living together.

117/ The scheme in England and Wales provided by three pieces of legislation which apply to different relationships and in different circumstances and give different relief presents even experienced lawyers with difficulties.

118/ See pages 56-57 and also the Report of the Committee on the London Metropolitan Police, 1986, unpublished.

119/ S. R. Moody and J. Tombs, Constructing Prosecution Decisions - The Case of the Procurator Fiscal (Scottish Academic Press, 1982), pp. 68-69.

120/ M.D.A. Freeman, "Violence against women: does the legal system provide solutions or itself constitute the problem?", British Journal of Law and Society, No. 7, 1980, p. 215. Dobash and Dobash, op. cit., pp. 217-218.

121/ Davis v. Johnson (1979) A.C. 264.

122/ K. McCann, "Battered women and the law: the limits of the legislation", Women in Law, J. Brophy and C. Smart, eds. (London, Routledge and Kegan Paul, 1985), p. 71.

123/ G. M. Thompson, "Resolution of domestic problems in the courtroom", in Domestic Violence: Issues and Dynamics, V. D'Oyley, ed. (Ontario Institute for Studies in Education, 1978) provides an account by a judge of the personal dilemmas he faced during cases of domestic assault.

124/ J. Hogarth, "Battered wives and the justice system" (Vancouver, University of British Columbia, Faculty of Law, 1979), unpublished, p. 24.

125/ L. G. Lerman, "The mediation of wife abuse cases: the adverse impact of informal dispute resolution on women", Harvard Women's Law Journal, No. 7, 1984, p. 61.

126/ Ibid., p. 90.

127/ Ibid., p. 91.

128/ Ibid., p. 68.

129/ Ibid., p. 86. Perhaps there is marginally less victimization in cases where the diversion occurs after arrest. Here, at least, the abuser, has become part of the criminal process, whereas if he is diverted prior to arrest there is no sanction at all.

130/ See Wu Han, case study from China (Shanghai, East China Institute of Law and Politics, Criminology and Crime Investigation Department). These groups play a mediating role and can, if necessary, refer the case to more stringent bodies, such as the public security department or the criminal justice department.

131/ See note 77.

132/ See case study from Uganda (Mukasa-Kikonyogo, op. cit.); Mediation may also be more appropriate and more respected in traditional communities which are part of multi-cultural societies. See, K. A. Long, "Cultural considerations in the assessment and treatment of intrafamilial abuse", American Journal of Orthopsychiatry, No. 56, 1986, p. 131. See also, the Australian case study which points out that Australian aboriginal women are very suspicious of solutions offered by the dominant culture (L'Orange, op. cit., p. 13).

133/ MacLeod quotes women who indicate that battered women are much happier with the criminal justice approach if there is some form of treatment package for the abuser built into the response (MacLeod, op. cit., p. 85).

134/ J. Pahl, "The general practitioner and the problems of battered women", Journal of Medical Ethics, No. 5, 1979, p. 117. Binney and others, op. cit. Dobash and Dobash, op. cit.

135/ Ibid., see also P. Jaffe and C. A. Burris, An Integrated Response to Wife Assault: A Community Model (Ottawa, Solicitor General of Canada, 1982).

136/ E. Hilberman and K. Munson, "Sixty battered women", Victimology, No. 2, 1977/78, p. 480. R. W. Swanson, "Battered wife syndrome", Canadian Medical Association Journal, No. 130, 1984, p. 709.

137/ Pagelow, op. cit., p. 140. Binney and others, op. cit., p. 20. Dobash and Dobash, op. cit., p. 181. Pahl, op. cit., 165.

138/ Dobash and Dobash, op. cit., p. 181.

139/ E. Stark, A. Flitcraft and W. Frazier, "Medicine and patriarchal wisdom: the social construction of a private event", International Journal of Health Services, No. 9, 1979, p. 466.

140/ The case study from Egypt relates the case of a woman abused so badly that she miscarried and was believed by the doctor to have caused her own mis-carriage (El Husseiny Zaalouk, op. cit., p. 28).

141/ J. Snell, R. J. Rosenwald and A. Robey, "The wife beater's wife", Archives of Gen. Psychiatry, No. 11, 1964, p. 107.

142/ M. Borkowski, M. Murch and V. Walker, Marital Violence: The Community Response (London, Tavistock, 1982), pp. 157-165.

143/ J. L. Herman, "Histories of violence in an outpatient population", American Journal of Orthopsychiatry, No. 56, 1986, p. 137.

144/ For example, Australian Law Reform Commission, Domestic Violence ....

145/ British Association of Social Workers, "Home violence - is there an answer?" Social Work Today, No. 6, 1975, pp. 409-413.

146/ Borkowski, Murch and Walker, op. cit., p. 89.

147/ N. Johnson, "Police, social work and medical responses to battered women", in Marital Violence, N. Johnson, ed. (London, Routledge and Kegan Paul, 1985), pp. 116-117. Pahl, op. cit., p. 125.

148/ Johnson, loc. cit., p. 117.

149/ Pahl, op. cit., p. 54.

150/ R. A. Berk, P. Newton and S. F. Berk, "What a difference a day makes: an empirical study of the impact of shelters for battered women", Journal of Marriage and the Family, No. 48, 1986, p. 483.

151/ Pahl, op. cit., p. 62.

152/ Note, however, in this context, the remarks of Morgan: "Refuges formerly run by small collectives of feminist activists, often with a strong community base, were replaced by larger service centres, administered by boards of directors and staffed by professionals ... Whereas once the aim was to educate women to live independent lives, it shifted towards family reunification" (P. A. Morgan, "Constructing deviance: a look at state intervention into the problem of wife battery", in Marital Violence, J. Johnson, ed. (London, Routledge and Kegan Paul, 1985), pp. 60 and 66).

153/ Food rules, for example, must be taken account of. In this context the refuge in Petaling Jaya, Malaysia housing Malay, Chinese and Indian women is a good example. Papachan, op. cit.

154/ MacLeod pinpoints the particular difficulties of aboriginal, immigrant and disabled women in refuges (MacLeod, op. cit., pp. 24-30).

155/ See Confronting Violence: A Manual for Commonwealth Action (London, Commonwealth Secretariat, Women and Development Programme, 1987), which includes a protocol for the establishment of a refuge.

156/ Australian Law Reform Commission, Domestic Violence ..., pp. 54-55.

157/ J. Browning, Stopping the Violence: Canadian Programmes for Assaultive Men (Health and Welfare Canada, 1984) indicates the models available in Canada and the United States.

158/ Ibid., p. 36.

159/ Ibid., p. 45. Anecdotal reports from group leaders suggest that the majority of the men, 75-100% are non-violent during the group meeting period and that up to about 55-60% remain non-violent up to four months after the therapy ends.

Part Three

WHAT CAN BE DONE

While the problem of violence against women in the home has appeared only recently as an issue of public concern and debate, it is clear that it is not a new phenomenon. All studies that exist indicate that wife abuse is a common and pervasive problem and that men from practically all countries, cultures, classes and income groups indulge in the behaviour. The issue has serious implications from both a short-term and long-term perspective and from an individual and societal perspective. Many victims suffer serious physical and psychological injury, sometimes even death, while the economic and social costs to the community are enormous and the implications for future generations impossible to estimate.

The cause of the conduct is not susceptible to easy definition. Clearly, the problem is complex and multifaceted and thus requires solutions that are similarly complex and multifaceted. Moreover, it must be appreciated that different solutions may be appropriate for different women and for different socio-cultural contexts.

I. CLEAR STRATEGIES

Although multiple factors contribute to violence against women in the home and the issue is a difficult one, it is not insoluble. Hence, for example, research has revealed a substantial drop in the incidence of violence against women in the home in the United States during the 10-year period from 1975 to 1985, a drop that the researchers attribute to a combination of changed attitudes and norms, together with changes in overt behaviour. Thus, the researchers point to the ameliorative effect of strategies introduced in the United States to confront family violence that have provided women with alternatives, and provided treatment and prevention service. Furthermore, they argue that the period has seen a marked swing away from the social acceptability of violence as a method of interpersonal relations in the family. 1/

The multifactorial nature of the problem of violence against women in the home indicates that it is an issue that must be approached from many perspectives and by many disciplines that do not act in isolation, but rather collaboratively. Any strategy to confront the problem must be compatible with the conditions and resources of the country under consideration. It is critical that all societies recognize the issue as a serious one and ensure that the behaviour is condemned by all those in authority, be they the State leaders, religious leaders or law enforcement agencies. Formal condemnation of itself, however, is insufficient. It must be accompanied by a clear manifestation of a resolution to act against the abuse, and to deal properly and effectively with both the victim and the abuser.

Improving responses to violence against women in the family will involve a number of strategies, crucial among which is the development of attitudes and values towards women in general, and wife assault in particular, that are based on the principles contained in the Nairobi Forward-looking Strategies and on accurate information rather than myths and stereotypes.

II. IMPROVED RESEARCH

The importance of research cannot be underrated. In many countries, research into the problem has not progressed beyond the most superficial. Even where research has been undertaken the information is often limited by the method of research or the research sample. Many studies, for example, use limited samples such as women in battered wives' shelters, police statistics, samples from counselling agencies and divorce statistics. Conclusions from such studies are thus based on surveys of small groups and of groups who come from partnerships that are already defined as troubled, or even violent, rather than from on-going functioning partnerships. There is a clear need for wider and deeper research so that the dynamics of family maltreatment can be understood more clearly.

Beyond the fact that research to determine the causes and dynamics of family maltreatment remains to be conducted, it is essential, also, that current strategies that have been introduced are specifically studied so that their effectiveness can be evaluated. Thus, little research has been under-taken into the effect of shelters in a community, or the effect a stay in a shelter or women's refuge may have on a woman's life.

Specific studies must be undertaken into the effectiveness of a criminal justice approach to wife assault as opposed to the welfare model. As yet, in those countries, such as Australia and Canada, where the criminal model has been opted for, the changes are very new and must still be regarded as experi-mental. It is important, therefore, to monitor and evaluate the effect of such an approach and the reforms in the system not only in terms of criminal statistics, but also in terms of their effect on battered women and their children, the batterers and service providers. As one commentator has put it:

"These evaluations should also ask some difficult questions. For example: Are we limiting the choices of some women through a too rigid application of criminal justice procedures (for example, charging women with contempt of court for refusing to testify against their partners)? Already some shelter workers speculate that because, under the law, children can be removed from a home where violence has occurred, women may be discouraged from reporting the violence. Is greater criminal justice intervention going to force some women back into hiding, particu-larly if women fear that this intervention will lead to the removal of the children? Could changes in operational guidelines for police, reached through consideration with child welfare and shelter workers, help allay this concern? It must also be asked: Do we want to bring more people to court?" 2/

Specific research is also required into the effect of bringing abuse cases into the family court, rather than the criminal court. Most importantly, research is particularly lacking on abusive men. Thus, the effectiveness of battering men's programmes must be analysed and evaluated and the violent men themselves must be studied, in order to determine how far their violence is the result of individual psychopathology or a result of social norms that condone and support subordination of women and thus male violence.

Any comprehensive measures to combat wife abuse must incorporate short-term and long-term measures. As wife abuse is perhaps best seen as a reflection of the unequal status of women in the family and society, it is clear that it will only disappear with long-term structural change. Thus,

short-term proposals may be greeted sceptically and may be accused of being
responses that deal only with symptoms rather than the underlying causes,
while proposals for fundamental change may be discarded as impractical or even
dangerous. None the less, wife abuse does raise immediate problems for people
working in a wide range of professions and fundamental questions on the nature
of gender relationships.

III. A MORE RESPONSIVE LEGAL SYSTEM

At the front line of response to the issue of wife abuse is the police. Police must develop adequate protocols to manage the problem and to act so that existing ambiguities or gaps in the law that deprive women of adequate legal recourse in cases of abuse are eliminated. Police practice must be improved and there must be a clear and explicit departmental policy indicating how wife assault should be treated. Ideally, this policy should indicate that wife assault is to be treated like assault in any other context and thus arrest and charge could be used. In recognition of the crucial role of police in the management of family violence, police at all levels should be provided with special training to provide them with greater understanding of the dynamics of the issue and to equip them in techniques of crisis intervention.

The assaulted woman must be given all assistance so that she has clear access to legal remedies should she wish to use them. Specific legal provisions which indicate that violence against women is excusable or tolerable must be repealed as must any provision discriminating on the basis of sex. Access to the courts must be simple and cheap. Any legal disability, such as considering women legally to be minors, that prevents a woman from bringing an action must be removed and any evidentiary barrier, such as provisions that prevent a woman giving evidence against her spouse, must be clarified.

Attitudes of legal personnel towards the legitimacy of wife assault charges, the seriousness of the activity and the attitude of the law towards women in general require scrutiny. It is most important that if any legal strategy is available for a woman who has been the subject of violence, all the actors involved, prosecutors, lawyers and judges, must implement it in the utmost good faith. There must be no gap between the law in theory and the law in practice.

While the law and its attendant actors are important factors in any strategy to confront violence against women in the home, it must be appreciated that improvement in legal remedies and legal services will be an insufficient response. Further, in some cases, legal strategies may be inappropriate. It cannot be stressed too greatly that each woman is different and each woman will require a different response. Further, some women may be positively harmed by an over-legal response to their situation. In the context of family violence, flexibility is essential and a rigid approach must be avoided so that the woman is not further victimized by the system.

The ultimate goal of any short-term measure to combat violence against women in the home must be to protect the individual woman. Her needs are safety, shelter, compassion, information and referral. She may require financial support, housing, help with her immigration status, the services of an interpreter, services for her children, counselling and assistance with the law. The individual woman should be able to take advantage of an integrated and co-ordinated service. It is important that she is not continually referred to another agency, thereby becoming lost in a bureaucratic maze, continually shunted between the health, legal and social sectors. Any response must involve an interrelationship between these sectors. Innovative strategies may be appropriate here. Thus, for example, the United States Task Force of Family Violence 3/ suggests there should be a "victim advocate" who could act as a focal point for the victim, telling her of the operation of the criminal justice system, referring her to appropriate agencies and keeping her informed of the progress of the case. A similar suggestion comes from the United Kingdom Committee on Violence in Marriage, 4/ which advocated the establishment of "family crisis centres" that would be open 24 hours per day, providing an emergency service, acting as a link between medical, social welfare and health services, and providing a focal point for women's shelters.

IV. EDUCATION

Short-term measures to combat violence against women must merge with long-term strategies. It is perhaps in the area of education and training that the link between short-term preventive and ameliorative measures and long-term strategies can be seen most clearly.

Many researchers subscribe to the view that wife assault is supported by the social structure and thus it will only be with change in that structure that the conduct will ultimately disappear. They believe, further, that long-term change in the social structure will only occur as a result of education. Education is the carrier of traditional norms and values and has played a crucial role in the crystallization of the female and male stereotype. As such, it has had a key role in the continued victimization of women. It can, however, act as a positive force for change and progress. Education must be used at various levels in the fight towards violence against women in the home.

Informal methods of education can be used to advise women of their available options and the support systems that exist and further, such informal methods can be used to convey the message to both women and men that the use of violence in family conflict resolution is inappropriate and must be deplored.

Education in schools from the primary stage of education must be geared to eliminate stereotypical social, economic and cultural roles of women and men. The subject of family violence should be part of family life education and methods of peaceful conflict resolution advocated. Steps towards this end have already been put in motion in Australia and Canada, where packages have been developed for school teachers for teaching about non-violence relation-ships. 5/

Further, attention must be paid to the particular national and cultural context so that appropriate and imaginative education strategies can be used. Thus, in some countries it may be appropriate to produce simple booklets, on the pattern, for example, of the excellent cartoon-style pamphlet published in Brazil. In other countries, poster campaigns may be appropriate. So, for example, Kenya mounted a national campaign placing posters in buses, railway stations, schools and other public places. Similarly, a poster display has been used in Malaysia, while, in China, city bulletin boards have displayed posters deploring abuse and indicating where a woman can receive help. Other countries, such as Jamaica, have taken advantage of the theatre to educate, while still others, appreciating the massive illiteracy in their communities, illiteracy that is usually greater among women, have relied on traditional forms of folk theatre. Thus, for example, special puppet shows have been produced in India deploring violence against women and the inferior position of women in the Indian family. 6/

Education must also be aimed at specific groups who are involved professionally with victims. Training for teachers, social workers, doctors, nurses and paramedics, the police, lawyers and the judiciary is essential. 7/ This training should encompass the dynamics of abuse, diagnosis, intervention, referrals and treatment. Further, training must be introduced into primary syllabuses and into service and refresher training.

The media is a powerful agent for education and social change. It has the capacity to preserve, record and define human culture and history. Currently, like education, it tends to project stereotypic images of women and

to support male values. It could, however, be used to foster sexual equality
and thus it could be a powerful agent in the fight against spouse abuse.

Research has not proven conclusively that there is a link between media
representations of violence and violence against women in the home, but it is
clear that the media does reflect cultural values and reinforces ideologies of
masculinity and femininity that demonstrate that while man is "naturally"
aggressive, woman is a "natural target" for the aggression. Thus, as Malamuth
and Donnerstein point out "... the overall pattern of the data strongly
supports the assertion that the mass media can contribute to a cultural climate
that is more accepting of aggression towards women". 8/ It is important thus
that the media act responsibly in the context of violence against women in the
home. Such violence should be deplored and not reported sensationally or
salaciously. Positive images of women, particularly focusing on female
equality and worth, should be fostered and encouraged.

V. ADDRESSING STRUCTURAL CAUSES

Clearly, therefore, there are a number of short-term approaches to the problem of violence against women in the home. A number of these strategies will have a long-term impact on the issue. Both short-term and long-term strategies will face obstacles. The current perception of violence against women in the family as a private problem is a serious barrier. So also is the view held by many women that any violence perpetrated against them by their spouses is a matter of shame and in some way provoked by their actions. These perceptions work to the batterer's advantage and are tacitly adopted by public authorities, such as doctors, social workers, the police, the legal profession and the judiciary, who join in a conspiracy of silence and in some way almost approve of the man's behaviour. Thus, as the Dobashes pointedly remark:

> "In a way the entire community ... is responsible for the continued assaults on women and in some cases their deaths: the friends and neighbours who ignore or excuse the violence, the physician who does not go beyond the mending of bones and the stitching of wounds, the social worker who defines wife beating as a failure of communication and the police and court officials who refuse to intervene. The violence is meted out by one man but the responsibility goes far beyond him." 9/

This responsibility must be accepted. The issue must be addressed publicly and in the most vehement of terms by those who lead and mould opinion. Non-formal agents of support, such as neighbours, friends and relatives, must be encouraged to intervene on the woman's behalf. Governments must allocate adequate resources to strategies that aim to deal with the issue.

Ultimately, however, the inferior status of women as opposed to that of men must be addressed. Violence against women in the family and elsewhere is the product of this inferiority, and the eradication of this violence will only occur if steps are taken to guarantee women equality in all spheres of life. Women must be assured of legal and financial independence, and they must be assured that there is no assumption of male domination within intimate relationships.

Violence against women is the product of the subordination of women. Short-term measures may have a short-term effect in context of spouse abuse without regard to the root cause of violence, but it is certain that no long-term measure will be successful unless there is a fundamental change in the social and economic structures that maintain the subordination of women within marriage and within wider society. Fundamental change is a complex question, but perhaps can be best begun if the ideals and goals of the Convention on the Elimination of All Forms of Discrimination against Women, as well as the principles and strategies contained in the Nairobi Forward-looking Strategies for the Advancement of Women to the Year 2000, are respected and implemented world-wide.

Notes

1/   M. Straus and R. J. Gelles, "Societal change in family violence from 1975 to 1985 as revealed by two national surveys", Journal of Marriage and the Family, No. 48, 1986, p. 465.

2/   L. MacLeod, Battered But Not Beaten (Ottawa, Canadian Advisory Council on the Status of Women, 1987), p. 90.

3/   Attorney-General's Task Force on Family Violence, Final Report (Washington, DC, Government Printer, 1984), p. 14.

4/   Report of the Select Committee of Violence in Marriage (London, HM Stationery Office, 1975), para. 20.

5/   See, for example, Ideas For Teaching About Non-Violent Relationships (New South Wales, Department of Education, Personal Development Unit, Directorate of Special Programs, 1984). W. Stojanowska, case study from Poland (Warsaw, Instytut Badania Prawa Sadowego, 1987), which describes the programme of education for family life which is run by the Society for the Development of the Family.

6/   Wu Han, case study from China (Shanghai, East China Institute of Law and Politics, Criminology and Crime Investigation Department, 1986), I. Shamim, case study from Bangladesh (Dhaka, University of Dhaka, Department of Sociology, 1987), D. Wood, case study from Canada (Ottawa, Social Policy at Status of Women Canada, 1987), K. N. Pryce, case study from Trinidad and Tobago (St. Augustine, University of the West Indies, 1986), B. N. Wamalwa, case study from Kenya (Nairobi, Public Law Institute, 1987), S. Skrobanek, case study from Bangladesh (Bangkok, Women's Information Centre, 1987).

7/   Note the case study from Greece by C. D. Spinellis (Athens, University of Athens, Faculty of Law, 1987), which indicates that a seminar for judges on domestic abuse was held in September 1987. Further, the Commonwealth Secretariat Women and Development Programme held an Expert Group Meeting of Law Teachers in London in May 1987 in order to work on the preparation of teaching materials on domestic violence and sexual assault against women to be used in law teaching in law schools and colleges through the Commonwealth.

8/   N. M. Malamuth and E. M. Donnerstein, Pornography and Sexual Aggression (New York, Academic Press, 1984).

9/   R. E. Dobash and R. Dobash, Violence Against Women: A Case Against the Patriarchy (London, Open Books, 1980), p. 222.

Bibliography

Adams, K. and J. Fay. No more secrets - protecting your child from sexual assault. San Luis Obispo, California, Impact Publishers, 1981.

Akanda, L. and I. Shamim. Women and violence: a comparative study of rural and urban violence in Bangladesh. Women's issue (Dhaka) 1:1, 1984.

Amir, M. Patterns in forcible rape. Chicago, University of Chicago Press, 1971.

Andrews, B. and G. W. Brown. Marital violence in the community: a biographical approach. British journal of psychiatry (London) 153:305, 1988.

Armstrong, L. Kiss daddy goodnight. New York, Pocket Books, 1978.

Atkins, S. and B. Hoggett. Women and the law. Oxford, Blackwell, 1985.

Attorney-General's Task Form on Family Violence. Final report. Washington, D.C., Government Printer, 1984.

Australian Law Reform Commission. Domestic violence in the Australian Capital Territory. A discussion paper. Canberra, A.G.P.S., 1984.

_____ Domestic violence. Report No. 30. Canberra, A.G.P.S, 1986.

Backhouse, C. and L. Cohen. The secret oppression: sexual harassment of working women. Toronto, MacMillan, 1978.

Bacon, L. and R. Landsdowne. Women who kill husbands - the problem of defence. Sydney, 52nd ANZAAS Conference, 1982.

The battered data syndrome: a comment on Steinmetz's article. By E. Pleck and others. Victimology (Arlington, Virginia) 2:680, 1978.

Bedfordshire police. Reports on acts of violence committed in the county between 1 February and 31 July 1976. Bedfordshire, 1976.

Bell, D. J. Domestic violence: victimization, police intervention and disposition. Journal of criminal justice (Elmsford, New York) 13:425, 1985.

Bell, D. A multi-year study of Ohio urban, suburban and rural police dispositions of domestic violence. Victimology (Arlington, Virginia) 10:301.

Bello, E. The status of women in Zimbabwe. Harare, 1985. Unpublished.

Bennett, T. W., ed. Family law in the last two decades of the twentieth century. Cape Town, Juta, 1983.

Berk, R. A. and P. J. Newton. Does arrest really deter wife-battery? An effort to replicate the findings of the Minneapolis Spouse Abuse Experiment. American sociological review (Washington, D.C.) 50:253, 1985.

Berk, R. A., P. J. Newton <u>and</u> S. F. Berk. What a difference a day makes: an empirical study of the impact of shelters for battered women. <u>Journal of marriage and the family</u> 48:481, 1986.

Berk, S. K. <u>and</u> D. R. Loseke. Handling family violence: situational determinants of police arrest in domestic disturbances. <u>Law and society review</u> (Denver, Colorado) 15:315, 1981.

Binney, V., G. Harkell <u>and</u> J. Nixon. Leaving violent men. London, Women's Aid Federation England, 1981.

Borkowski, M., M. Murch <u>and</u> V. Walker. Marital violence: the community response. London, Tavistock, 1982.

Borland, M., <u>ed</u>. Violence in the family. Manchester, Manchester University Press, 1976.

Bowker, L. H. Beating wife-beating. Lexington, Mass., Lexington Books, 1983.

Boyle, C. Sexual assault. Toronto, Carswells, 1984.

Brienes, W. <u>and</u> L. Gordon. The new scholarship on family violence. <u>Signs: journal of women in culture and society</u> 8:490, 1983.

British Association of Social Workers. Home violence: is there an answer? <u>Social work today</u> (Birmingham) 6:409, 1975.

Brophy, J. <u>and</u> C. Smart, <u>eds</u>. Women in law: explorations in law, family and sexuality. London, Routledge and Kegan Paul, 1985.

Brown, S. E. Police responses to wife beating: neglect of a crime of violence. <u>Journal of criminal justice</u> (Elmsford, New York) 12:277, 1984.

Browning, J. Stopping the violence: Canadian programmes for assaultive men. Ottawa, National Health and Welfare Canada, 1984.

Brownmiller, S. Against our will. New York, Bantam Books, 1975.

California Commission on the Status of Women. Domestic violence fact sheet. Sacramento, California, 1978.

Canadian Council on Social Development. Mental health assistance to victims of crime and their families. Report on the victims' trauma conference. Ottawa, 1985.

Cannings, D. M. Myths and stereotypes: obstacles to effective police intervention in domestic disputes. <u>Police journal</u> (Chichester, Sussex) 43-56, 1984.

Chambers, G. <u>and</u> A. Millar. Investigating sexual assault. Edinburgh, H.M. Stationery Office, 1983.

Chapman, J. R. <u>and</u> M. Gates, <u>eds</u>. The victimization of women. Beverly Hills, California, Sage. 1982.

Chester, R. <u>and</u> J. Strether. Cruelty in English divorce: some empirical findings. <u>Journal of marriage and the family</u> (St. Paul, Minnesota) 34:706, 1972.

Children of battered women: the relation of child behaviour to family
    violence and maternal stress. <u>By</u> D. A. Wolfe <u>and others</u>. <u>Journal of
    consulting and clinical psychology</u> (Washington, D.C.) 53:657, 1985.

Church, R. J. Violence against wives: its causes and effects: results of
    the Christchurch family violence study. Christchurch, New Zealand,
    Battered Women's Support Group, 1984.

_____ How to get out of your marriage alive. Christchurch, New Zealand,
    Battered Women's Support Group, 1978.

Church, R. J. <u>and</u> D. E. Church. Listen to me please! The legal needs of
    domestic violence victims. Christchurch, New Zealand, Battered Women's
    Support Group, 1982.

Clark, L.M.G. <u>and</u> D. Lewis. Rape: the price of coercive sexuality. Toronto,
    Women's Educational Press, 1977.

Cobbe, F. Wife torture in England. <u>Contemporary review</u> (London), April 1878.

Committee on Sexual Offences Against Children and Youths. Sexual offences
    against children. Ottawa, Supply and Services, 1984.

Connell, N. <u>and</u> C. Wilson, <u>eds</u>. Rape: the first sourcebook for women.
    New York, New American Library, 1974.

d'Abbs, P. Domestic violence between adults in the Northern Territory.
    Melbourne, Institute of Family Studies, 198..

The dark side of families. <u>By</u> D. Finkelhor, <u>ed</u> , <u>and others</u>. Beverly Hills,
    Sage, 1983.

Davidson, T. Conjugal crime: understanding and changing the wife beating
    pattern. New York, Ballantine Books, 1978.

Dawson, B. <u>and</u> T. Faragher. Battered women's project. Interim report.
    Keele, United Kingdom, University of Keele, Department of Sociology, 1977.

Department of Education. The Law Society of Upper Canada. For the family law
    practitioner: how to represent the battered client.
        Prepared for a programme held at Toronto, 22 November 1986.

Dobash, R. E. <u>and</u> R. Dobash. The nature and antecedents of violent events.
    <u>British journal of crime</u> 24:629, 1984.

_____ Violence against wives: a case against the patriarchy. London,
    Open Books, 1980.

_____ Violence against wives in Scotland. Research Report for the
    Scottish Home and Health Department. Edinburgh, 1979.

_____ Wife beating. <u>Social work today</u> (Birmingham) 14, 1977.

_____ Wife beating – the negotiation of daily life under patriarchal
    domination. Research paper. University of Stirling, Department of
    Sociology, Scotland.

_____ Wives: the "appropriate" victims of marital violence. <u>Victimology</u> (Arlington, Virginia) 2:426, 1977/78.

Domestic Violence Committee. Report. Sydney, New South Wales Government Printer, 1985.

Downey, J. <u>and</u> J. Howell. Wife battering - a review and preliminary enquiry into local incidents, needs and resources. Vancouver, National Department of Health and Welfare, 1976.

D'Oyley, V., <u>ed</u>.. Domestic violence: issues and dynamics. Ontario, Ontario Institute for Studies in Education, 1978.

Dworkin, A. Our blood. London, Women's Press, 1981.

_____ Pornography: men possessing women. London, Women's Press, 1977.

Eddy, M. <u>and</u> T. Myer. Helping men who batter: a profile of programs in the U.S. Texas, Texas Department of Human Resources, 1984.

Edwards, S. Compelling a reluctant spouse: policing and the prosecution process. <u>New law journal</u> (London), November 1985.

_____ Female sexuality and the law. Oxford, Robertson, 1981.

_____ The police response to domestic violence in London. Interim report. London, 1986.
    Unpublished.

_____ When is a crime a "crime"? Domestic violence and policing in London. A paper presented to the European Conference of Critical Legal Studies, University of London, 3-5 April 1986.

Edwards, S., <u>ed</u>. Gender, sex and the law. London, Croom Helm, 1985.

Eekelaar, J. Family law and social policy. London, Weidenfeld and Nicolson, 1984.

Eekelaar, J. M. <u>and</u> S. N. Katz, <u>eds</u>. Family violence: an international and interdisciplinary study. Toronto, Butterworths, 1978.

Eisenberg, S. <u>and</u> P. Miclow. The assaulted wife: catch 22 revisited. <u>Women's rights law reporter</u> (Cambridge, Mass.) 3:138, 1977.

Emotional and physical health problems of battered women. <u>By</u> P. Jaffe <u>and</u> <u>others</u>. <u>Canadian journal of psychiatry</u> (Ottawa) 31:625, 1986.

Epstein, R., Ng, R. <u>and</u> M. Trebble. The social organization of family violence: an ethnography of immigrant experience in Vancouver. Vancouver, Women's Research Center, 1978.

Evason, E. Hidden violence: a study of battered women in Northern Ireland. Belfast, Farset Co-operative Press, 1982.

Farley, L. Sexual shakedown: the sexual harassment of women on the job. New York, Warner Books, 1978.

Faulk, M. Men who assault their wives. Medicine, science and the law (London) 14:183, 1974.

Federal/provincial/territorial report on wife battering to the ministers responsible for the status of women. Niagara-on-the-Lake, Canada, Ministry of Supply, 1984.

Federal/Provincial/Territorial Working Group on Wife Battering. Final report. Ministry of Supply, Canada, 1986.

Fields, M. D. Wife beating: government intervention policies and practices. In Battered women: issues of public policy. Washington, D.C., US. Government Printing Office, 1978.

Fields, M. D. and R. M. Kirchner. Battered women are still in need: a reply to Steinmetz. Victimology (Arlington, Virginia) 3:216, 1978.

Finkelhor, D. Sexually victimized children. New York, Free Press, 1979.

Fischer, D. G. Family relationship variables and programs influencing juvenile delinquency. Ottawa, Solicitor-General of Canada, 1985.

Fleming, J. B. Stopping wife abuse. Anchor Press, 1979.

Foakes, J. Family violence: law and practice. London, Hemstal Press, 1984.

Freeman, M.D.A. "Le vice anglais? - wife battering in English and American law" Family law quarterly (Agincourt, Ontario) 11:199, 1977.

_____ Violence against women: does the legal system provide solutions or itself constitute the problem? British journal of law and society (Oxford) 7:215, 1980.

_____ Violence in the home. Farnborough, Saxon House, 1979

Friend, R. Eva. Melbourne, McPhea Gribble, Penguin, 1985.

Frieze, I. H. Investigating the causes and consequences of marital rape. Signs: journal of women in culture and society 8:532, 1983.

Galen, D. P. Internal conflicts between customary law and general law in Zimbabwe: family law as a case study. Zimbabwe law review 1:3, 1983.

Ganley, A. L. Court mandated counselling for men who batter. Washington, D.C., Center for Women Policy Studies, 1981.

Gayford, J. J. Aetiology of wife beating. Medicine, Science and the law 19:19, 1979.

_____ Battered wives. Medicine, science and the law 15:237, 1975.

_____ Ten types of battered women. Welfare officer (Manchester) 25, 1976.

_____ Wife battering: a preliminary survey of 100 cases. British medical journal (London) 1:194, 1975.

Gee, P. W. Ensuring police protection for battered women: the Scott v. Hart suit. Signs: journal of women in culture and society 8:554, 1983.

Geis, G. Rape in marriage and law reform in England, the U.S. and Sweden. Adelaide law review (Adelaide) 6:284, 1978.

Gelles, R. J. Abused wives: why do they stay? Journal of marriage and the family (St. Paul, Minnesota) 39:15, 1979.

_____ Child abuse as psychopathology: a sociological critique and reformation. American journal of orthopsychiatry (New York) 43:43, 1973.

_____ Family violence. Sage, Beverly Hills, 1979.

_____ Power, sex and violence: the case of marital rape. The family co-ordinator (St. Paul, Minnesota) 26:339, 1977.

_____ Violence in the family: a review of research in the seventies. Journal of marriage and the family (St. Paul, Minnesota) 42, 1980.

_____ The violent home. Beverly Hills, California, Sage, 1972.

Ghent, W. R., N. P. Da Sylva and M. E. Farren. Family violence: guidelines for recognition and management. Canadian medical association journal (Ottawa) 132:541, 1985.

Gibson, E. and S. Klein. Murder 1957-1968: a Home Office statistical division report on murder in England and Wales, London, H.M. Stationery Office, 1969.

Giles-Sims, J. Wife battering: a systems theory approach. New York, Guilford Press, 1983.

Goldsberry, N. Rape in British Columbia: a report to the Ministry of the Attorney-General. British Columbia, Justice Development Commission, 1979.

Goode, W. J. Force and violence in the family. Journal of marriage and the family (St. Paul, Minnesota) 33:624, 1971.

Griffin, S. Pornography and silence. London, Women's Press, 1981.

_____ Rape: the power of consciousness. San Francisco, Harper and Row, 1979

Hadjifotiou, N. Women and harassment at work. London, Pluto Press, 1983.

Hancock, M. Battered women: an analysis of women and domestic violence. Wellington, New Zealand, The Committee on Women, 1979.

Harvey, W. and A. Watson-Russell. So you have to go to court. A child's guide to testifying as witness in child abuse cases. Scarborough, Canada, Butterworths.

Hedlund, E., ed. Rape: a drama from two perspectives. Report of a European seminar organized by the Swedish Association of Sex Education, Tynnigo. I.P.P.F., Sweden, 1985.

Helfer, R. E. and C. H. Kempe, eds. Child abuse and neglect: the family and the community. Cambridge, Mass., Ballinger, 1976.

Herman, J. L. Histories of violence in an outpatient population. American journal of orthopsychiatry (New York) 137, 1986.

Herman, J. Father/daughter incest. Harvard, Mass., Harvard University Press, 1981.

Hilberman, E. The rape victim. New York, Basic Books, 1976.

Hilberman, E. and K. Munson. Sixty battered women. Victimology (Arlington, Virginia) 2:460, 1978.

Hirschon, R. Women and property: women as property. London, Croom Helm, 1984

Hogarth, J. Battered wives and the justice system. Vancouver, University of British Columbia, Faculty of Law, 1979.
     Unpublished.

Holmes, S. A Detroit model for police-social work co-operation. Social casework (Milwaukee, Wisconsin) 64:220, 1982.

Holmstrom, L. L. and A. W. Burgess. The victim of rape: institutional reactions. New York, John Wiley, 1978.

Homicidally aggressive young children: neuropsychiatric and experimental correlates. By D. O. Lewis and others. American journal of psychiatry (Washington, D.C.) 140:148.

Hong, E., ed. Malaysian women: problems and issues. Penang, Consumers' Association of Penang, 1983.

Honore, T. Sex law. London, Duckworth, 1978.

Hough, A. and P. Mayhew. The British crime survey. London, H.M. Stationery Office. (Home Office Research Study, No. 76)

House of Commons. Report of the Select Committee on Violence in Marriage. London, H.M. Stationary Office, 1975.

Hughes, H. M. and S. J. Barad. Psychological functioning of children in a battered women's shelter: a preliminary investigation. American journal of orthopsychiatry (New York) 53:525, 1983.

Humphreys, J. C. and W. Humphreys. Mandatory arrest: a means of primary and secondary prevention of abuse of female partners. Victimology (Arlington, Virginia) 267, 1985.

The impact of the police laying charges in incidents of wife abuse. By P. Jaffe and others. Journal of family violence (New York) 1:37, 1986.

Jackson, S. and P. Rushton. Victims and villains: images of women in accounts of family violence. Women's studies international forum (Elmsford, New York) 5:17, 1982.

Jackson, T. L. and G. Sandberg. Attribution of incest blame among rural attorneys and judges. Women and therapy (New York) 4:39, 1985.

Jaffe, P. and C. A. Burris. An integrated response to wife assault: a community model. Ottawa, Solicitor-General of Canada, 1982.

_____ Wife abuse as a crime: the impact of police laying charges. Canadian journal of criminology (Ottawa) 25:309, 1983.

Jaffe, P., S. Wilson and D. A. Wolfe. Promoting changes in attitudes and understanding of conflict resolution among child witnesses of family violence. Canadian journal of behavioral science 18:356, 1986.

Jayaratne, L. Child abusers as parents and children. Social work 22, 1977.

Johnson, N. Marital violence. London, Routledge and Kegan Paul, 1985.

Klein, D. Violence against women: some considerations regarding its causes and its elimination. Crime and delinquency (Newbury Park, California) 27:64, 1981.

Langley, R. and R. C. Levy. Wifebeating: the silent crisis. New York, Kangaroo Book, 1978.

Law Reform Commission of Canada. Report on sexual offences. Ottawa, Law Reform Commission of Canada, 1978.

Law Reform Commission of Papua New Guinea. Domestic violence in Papua New Guinea. Boroko, Law Reform Commission, 1985. (Monograph No. 3)

_____ Interim report on domestic violence. Boroko, Law Reform Commission, 1987.

_____ Marriage and domestic violence in rural Papua New Guinea. Boroko, Law Reform Commission, 1985. (Occasional Paper No. 18)

_____ Marriage and domestic violence in urban Papua New Guinea. Boroko, Law Reform Commission, 1986. (Occasional Paper No. 19)

Law School, University of Strathclyde. Operating the Matrimonial Homes Act: the first six months. Research Report. University of Strathclyde, 1983.

Lederer, L., ed. Take back the night: women on pornography. New York, William Morrow, 1983.

Lefcourt, C. H., ed. Women and the law. New York, Clark Boardman, 1984.

Leonard, R. and E. Macleod. Marital violence: social construction and social service response. Warwick, United Kingdom, University of Warwick, 1980.

Lerman, L. G. Mediation of wife abuse cases: the adverse impact of informal dispute resolution on women. Harvard women's law journal (Cambridge, Mass.) 7:57, 1984.

Leving, G. Source of marital dissatisfaction among applicants for divorce. American journal of orthopsychiatry (New York) 36:80, 1966.

Littlejohn, G., ed. Power and the state. London, Croom Helm, 1977.

Livneh, E. On rape and the sanctity of matrimony. Israel law review (Jerusalem) 2:425, 1967.

London Rape Crisis Centre. Sexual violence: the reality for women. London, Women's Press, 1984.

London Strategic Policy Unit, Police Monitoring and Research Group. Police response to domestic violence. Briefing paper No. 1. London, London Strategic Policy Unit, 1986.

Long, K. A. Cultural considerations in the assessment and treatment of intrafamilial abuse. American journal of orthopsychiatry (New York) 56:131, 1986.

McClintock, F. H. Crimes of violence. London, MacMillan, 1963.

MacDonald, J. H. Rape: offenders and their victims. Illinois, Thomas, 1971.

MacKinnon, C. A. Sexual harassment of working women: a case of sex discrimination. New Haven, Connecticut, Yale University Press, 1979.

MacLeod, L. Wife battering in Canada: the vicious circle. Quebec, Canadian Government Publishing Centre, 1980.

_____ Battered but not beaten: preventing wife battering in Canada. Ottawa, Canadian Advisory Committee on the Status of Women. 1987.

Mcleod, M. Victim non co-operation in domestic disputes. Criminology (Columbus, Ohio) 21:395, 1983.

Maidment, S. The law's response to marital violence in England and the U.S.A. International and comparative law quarterly (London) 405, 1977.

_____ The relevance of the criminal law to domestic violence. Journal of social welfare law (London) 26, 1980.

Malamuth, N. M. and E. M. Donnerstein. Pornography and sexual aggression. New York, Academic Press, 1984.

Marsh, J. C., A. Geist and N. Caplan. Rape and the limits of law reform. Boston, Mass., Auburn House, 1982.

Martin, D. Battered wives. New York, Kangaroo Book, 1977.

Martin, J. P., ed. Violence and the family. New York, John Wiley, 1978.

Mill, J. S. The subjection of women. London, Virago, 1983.

Mitchell, M. H. Does wife abuse justify homicide? Wayne law review (Detroit, Michigan) 24:1705, 1978.

Montgomery, P. and V. Bell. Police response to wife assault: a Northern Ireland study. Belfast, Northern Ireland Women's Aid Federation, 1986.

Moody, S. R. and J. Tombs. Constructing prosecution decisions - the case of the procurator fiscal. Edinburgh, Scottish Academic Press. 1983

Naffin, N. An inquiry into the substantive law of rape. Adelaide, Women's Adviser's Office, Department of Premier and Cabinet, 1984.

_____ Domestic violence and the law. Adelaide, Government Printer, 1985.

National Clearing House on Domestic Violence. Wife abuse in the medical
    setting: an introduction for health personnel. Washington, D.C., 1981.

Nelson, S. Incest: fact not fiction. Stramullion Press, 1981.

New South Wales Department of Education, Directorate of Special Programs.
    Ideas for teaching about non-violent relationships. New South Wales, 1984.

New South Wales Domestic Violence Committee. Report, April 1983-June 1985.
    Sydney, Government Printer, 1985.

New South Wales Government. Violence Against Women and Children Law Reform
    Task Force. Consultation paper. New South Wales, Government Printer, 1987.

New South Wales Task Force on Domestic Violence. Report. Sydney, Government
    Printer, 1981.

O'Brian, J. Violence in divorce prone families. _Journal of marriage and the_
    family (St. Paul, Minnesota) 33:692, 1971.

O'Donnell, C. _and_ J. Craney, _eds_. Family violence in Australia. Melbourne,
    Longman Cheshire, 1982.

Oppenlander, N. Coping or copping out. _Criminology_ (Columbus, Ohio) 20:449,
    1982.

Pagelow, M. Battered women: a new perspective. Dublin, International
    Sociological Association, 1977.

_____ Woman-battering: victims and their experiences. Beverly Hills, Sage,
    1981.

Pahl, J. The general practitioner and the problems of battered women.
    Journal of medical ethics (London) 5:117, 1979.

_____ Police response to battered women. _Journal of social welfare law_
    (London) 337, 1982.

_____ A refuge for battered women. London, H.M. Stationery Office, 1978.

Pahl, J., _ed_. Private violence and public policy: the needs of battered
    women and the response of the public services. London, Routledge and Kegan
    Paul, 1985.

Parnas, R. Police discretion and diversion in incidents of intra-family
    problems. _Law and contemporary problems_ (Durham, North Carolina) 36:539,
    1971.

_____ Police response to domestic disturbance. _Wisconsin law review_ (Madison,
    Wisconsin) 914, 1967.

Phillips, A. _and_ H. P. Morris. _Marriage laws in Africa_. Oxford, Oxford
    University Press, 1971.

Pizzey, E. Scream quietly or the neighbours will hear. Hamondsworth, United
    Kingdom, Penguin Books, 1979.

Pizzey, E. and J. Shapiro. Prone to violence. London, Hamlyn, 1982.

Pleck, E. Feminist responses to "Crimes against women" 1858-1896. Signs: journal of women in culture and society 8:451, 1983.

Potts, D. and S. Herzerberger. Child abuse: a cross generational pattern of child rearing? Paper presented at the Annual Meeting of Midwest Psychological Association. Chicago, 1979.

The public and the private. By E. Gamarnikow, ed., and others. London, Heineman, 1983.

Punch, M., ed. Control in the police organization. London, MIT Press, 1983.

The rapist who pays the rent. 2. ed. By R. Hall and others. Bristol, Falling Wall Press, 1984.

Read, S. Sexual harassment at work. London, Hamlyn, 1982.

Renvoize, J. Web of violence: a study of family violence. London, Routledge and Kegan Paul, 1978.

_____ Incest: a family pattern. London, Routledge and Kegan Paul, 1982.

Report of the Working Party of the London Metropolitan Police. London, 1986. Unpublished.

Rowland, J. Rape: the ultimate violation. London, Pluto Press, 1985.

Roy, M. Battered women. New York, Van Nostrand Reinhold, 1977.

_____ The abusive partner. New York, Van Nostrand Reinhold, 1982.

Rush, F. The best kept secret: sexual abuse of children. Englewood Cliffs, Prentice-Hall, 1980.

Russell, D.E.H. The politics of rape. New York, Stein and Day, 1975.

_____ Rape in marriage. New York, Collier Books, 1982.

Russell, J. S., ed. A feminist review of criminal law. Canada, Minister of Supply and Services, 1985.

Schechter, S. Women and male violence: the visions and struggles of the battered women's movement. London, Pluto Press, 1982.

Scottish Law Commission. Report on occupancy rights in the matrimonial home. Law Com. No. 6. Edinburgh, H.M. Stationery Office, 1980.

Scutt, J. Consent in rape: the problem of the marriage contract. Monash law review (Clayton, Victoria, Australia) 3:257, 1977.

_____ Even in the best of homes: violence in the family. Ringwood, Victoria, Australia, Pelican Books, 1983.

_____ Going backwards: law "Reform" and woman bashing. Women's studies international forum (Elmsford, New York) 9:49, 1986.

Scutt, J., ed. Violence in the family. Canberra, Australian Institute of Criminology, 1980.

Sedley, A. and M. Benn. Sexual harassment at work. London, N.C.C.L. Rights of Women Unit, 1982.

Sexual assault of children and adolescents. By A. Burgess and others. Lexington, Mass., Lexington Books, 1981.

Shamim, I. Kidnapped, raped, killed: recent trends in Bangladesh families in the face of urbanisation. New Delhi Conference on Violence Against Women: New Delhi, 2-5 December 1985

Sherman, L. W. and R. A. Berk. The specific deterrent effects of arrest for domestic assault. American sociological review (Washington, D.C.) 49:261, 1984.

Shulman, M. A survey of spousal abuse against women in Kentucky. New York, Louis Harris, 1979.

Similarities in behavioral and social maladjustment among child victims and witnesses to family violence. By P. Jaffe and others. American journal of orthopsychiatry (New York) 56:142, 1986.

Sinclair, D., ed. Understanding wife assault. A training manual for counsellors and advocates. Toronto, Ontario Government Bookstore Publications Services, 1985.

Smart, C. and B. Smart, eds. Women, sexuality and social control. London, Routledge and Kegan Paul, 1978.

Snell, J., R. J. Rosenwald, and A. Robey. The wife beater's wife. Archives of general psychiatry (Chicago) 11:107, 1964.

A sourcebook on child sexual abuse. By Finkelhor, D. and others. Beverly Hills, Sage, 1986.

Srinivas, M. N. Some reflections on dowry. Oxford, Oxford University Press, 1984.

Stacey, W. and A. Shupe. The family secret: domestic violence in America. Boston, Beacon Press, 1983.

Stanko, E. A. Intimate intrusions: women's experience of male violence. London, Routledge and Kegan Paul, 1985.

Stark, E., A. Flitcraft, and W. Frazier. Medicine and patriarchial wisdom: the social construction of a private event. International journal of health services (Farmingdale, New York) 9:466, 1979.

Steinmetz, S. K. The battered husband syndrome. Victimology (Arlington, Virginia) 2:499, 1978.

_____ The cycle of violence: assertive, aggressive and abusive family interaction. New York, Praeger, 1977.

_____ Women and violence: victims and perpetrators. American journal of psychotherapy (New York) 34:334, 1980.

Steinmetz, S. K. and M. Straus, eds. Violence in the family. New York, Dodd and Mead, 1974.

Storr, A. Human aggression. London, Penguin, 1974.

Straus, M. Wife beating: how common and why? Victimology (Arlington, Virginia) 2:443, 1978.

Straus, M. and R. J. Gelles. Societal change in family violence from 1975 to 1985 as revealed by two national surveys. Journal of marriage and the family (St. Paul, Minnesota) 48:465, 1986.

Straus, M., R. J. Gelles, and S. K. Steinmetz. Behind closed doors: violence in the American family. New York, Anchor Books, 1980.

Straus, M. and G. Hotaling, eds. The social causes of husband-wife violence. Minneapolis, University of Minnesota Press, 1980.

Swanson, R. W. Battered wife syndrome. Canandian medical association journal (Ottawa) 130:709, 1984.

Tahourdin, B. Family violence. International journal of offender therapy and criminology (Portland, Oregon) 27:79, 1983.

Task Force on Spousal Assault. Final report, prepared for the minister responsible for the status of women, Government of the North West Territories. Yellowknife, Canada, 1985.

Toft, S., ed. Domestic violence in Papua New Guinea. Boroko, Papua New Guinea Law Reform Commission, 1986. (Monograph 3)

Toner, B. The facts of rape. London, Hutchinson, 1977

Tong, R. Women, sex and the law. Rowman and Allanheld, Totowa, New Jersey, 1984.

United Nations. Economic Commission for Africa. African Training and Research Centre for Women. Law and the status of women in Nigeria. Prepared by J. O. Akande, 1979.

United States Commission on Civil Rights Consultation. Battered wives: issues of public policy. Washington, 1978.

United States Department of Justice, Bureau of Justice Statistics. Intimate victims: a study of violence among friends and relations, 1980.

United States Department of Justice, Federal Bureau of Investigation. Uniform crime reports. Washington, D.C., U.S. Government Printing Office, 1985.

United States President's Commission on Law Enforcement and the Administration of Justice. Task Force Report. Crime and its impact: an assessment. Washington, D.C., U.S. Government Printing Office, 1967.

Von Hentig, H. The criminal and his victim. New Haven, Connecticut, Shoe String, 1948.

Waits, K. The criminal justice system's response to battering: understanding the problem: forging the solutions. <u>Washington law review</u> (Seattle, Washington) 60:267, 1985.

Walker, L. The battered woman. New York, Harper and Row, 1979.

_____ Psychological impact of the criminalization of domestic violence on victims. <u>Victimology</u> (Arlington, Virginia) 10:281, 1985.

Warrior, B. Battered women's directory. 9. ed. Richmond, Earlham College.

Wasik, M. Cumulative provocation and domestic killing. <u>Criminal law review</u> (London) 29, 1982.

Wasoff, F. Legal protection from wife beating: the processing of domestic assaults by the Scottish prosecutors and criminal courts. <u>International journal of the sociology of law</u> (London) 10:187, 1982.

Watt, D. The new offences against the person: the provisions of bill C-127. Toronto, Butterworths, 1984.

Wife Assault Implementation Team, Province of British Columbia. Wife assault information kit. Victoria, British Columbia, 1986.

Wilson, E. The existing research into battered women. London, National Women's Aid Federation, 1976.

_____ What is to be done about violence against women? London, Penguin, 1984.

Wilt, M. <u>and</u> R. K. Breedlove. Domestic violence and the police: studies in Detroit and Kansas City. Washington, Police Foundation, 1977.

Wolfgang, M. E. Patterns in criminal homicide. Philadelphia, University of Pennsylvania Press, 1958.

Women and Development Programme. Commonwealth Secretariat. Confronting violence. London, 1987.

Women's National Commission. Violence against women: Report of an Ad-Hoc Working Group. London, H.M. Stationery Office, 1984.

Woods, L. Litigation on behalf of battered women. <u>Women's rights law reporter</u> (Cambridge, Mass.) 18:18, 1978.

Worden, R. E. <u>and</u> A. A. Pollitz. Police arrests in domestic disturbances: a further look. <u>Law and society review</u> (Denver, Colorado) 18:105, 1984.

Yllo, K. <u>and</u> D. Finkelhor. Licence to rape: sexual abuse of wives. New York, Holt Reinhart and Winston, 1985.